ART, HEALING, and TRANSFORMATION

# PULSE
## ART, HEALING, and TRANSFORMATION

STEIDL / THE INSTITUTE OF CONTEMPORARY ART, BOSTON

## PREFACE

Current intellectual debates in science, philosophy, politics, and culture are grappling with new approaches to healing and their social and moral implications as well as their practical application. Medical advances in understanding the mind-body connection and the economic and political issues that dominate healthcare are a few of the social realities that shape ideas of wellness in individual lives and whole communities. As contemporary life is increasingly shaped by confrontations with illness and treatment, the idea of healing as distinct from cure is increasingly relevant. The therapeutic role of art in health and healing and the contemporary artist's response to this landscape are the themes of the exhibition, *Pulse: Art, Healing, and Transformation*, and this accompanying publication.

The role of the visual and performing arts in healing has antecedents ranging from the creation of Buddhist tankas and Tibetan mandelas to the use of Navajo rugs and chants to treat mental illness. Florence Nightingale, in her 1859 book *Notes on Nursing: What It Is and What It Is Not*, wrote, "Little as we know about the way we are affected by form: by color and light, we do know this, they have an actual physical effect. Variety of form and brilliancy of color in the objects presented to patients are actual means of recovery. People say the effect is only on the mind. It is no such thing. The effect is on the body, too."

Early twentieth-century artists such as Matisse and Franz Marc explicitly sought to provide psychological comfort through their art. Marc's letter to August Macke in 1911 demonstrates the ambitions of many of the Blaue Reiter artists to purposely effect change: "We have hopes for so much [that is] healing and inspirational from it." Later in the century, the pioneering figures of Lygia Clark in Brazil and Joseph Beuys in Germany sought to heal individuals, in the case of Clark, and German society in the case of Beuys through their artistic practice.

*Pulse* presents the work of Clark and Beuys as the historic foundation for the work of contemporary artists whose imagery and processes explore the role of ritual, narrative, metaphor, and movement to advance healing. We are grateful to each of the artists: Gretchen Bender; Bill T. Jones; Tania Bruguera; Cai Guo-Qiang; Irene and Christine Hohenbüchler; Wolfgang Laib; David Medalla; Ernesto Neto; and Richard Yarde; to the estates of Felix Gonzalez-Torres; Leonilson; and Hannah Wilke; and to our lenders for participating in this exhibition.

The ability to undertake an exhibition of this magnitude was quite literally made possible by the early and generous support of the Emily Hall Tremaine Foundation. We also received major support from the Andy Warhol Foundation and the Goethe Institut, Boston. We are very grateful for the confidence and commitment of our philanthropic partners.

The essays of Sandra Alvarez de Toledo, Thierry Davila, Gwendolyn DuBois Shaw, Sander Gilman, and Jessica Morgan make an important and lasting contribution to the catalogue and to the discourse and debate on art, psychology, politics, and medicine. We extend our appreciation for their work and welcome the new collaboration with our co-publisher Steidl.

At the ICA, Jessica Morgan undertook the organization of this exhibition and publication. Her insight and focus were responsible for framing and shaping this complex artistic and intellectual inquiry. She was ably assisted by Nora Donnelly, Registrar; Ena Fox, Director of Education; Carole Anne Meehan, ICA/Vita Brevis Project Director; Emily Moore, Curatorial Assistant; Tim Obetz, Exhibitions Manager; and Gilbert Vicario, Assistant Curator, and I thank each of them for their contribution.

*Pulse: Art, Transformation, and Healing* demonstrates the power of art and the creative process as a transformative agent for change. We are very proud to bring this exhibition and publication to life.

Jill Medvedow, James Sachs Plaut Director

## ACKNOWLEDGEMENTS

This catalogue and the exhibition that occasioned it are the result of a number of years' work that required the contribution of many people. At the ICA, all members of staff have contributed to this ambitious project but in particular I would like to thank Jill Medvedow, Director, for helping to initiate the concept for the exhibition and challenging me at all stages of its development to maintain our original vision. Emily Moore has worked enthusiastically and with keen attention to realize the exhibition as well as contributing eloquently to the biographies and handling the overall coordination for the catalogue. Branka Bogdanov, Nora Donnelly, Tim Obetz, and Gilbert Vicario have all helped both to arrange loans, facilitate the development of new works, and to install the exhibition, for which I thank them. Ena Fox and Carole Anne Meehan worked with me to organize our first advisory committee for this exhibition; I thank those who participated in these highly informative events and Ena and Carole Anne for their outstanding work in education and public art programming.

During the planning of the exhibition I received welcome advice and research help from a number of people, and I would like to thank in particular Guy Brett, Pablo Helguera, Ulrich Lehmann, Peter Nisbet, Beeke Sell-Tower, and Caroline Tisdall. The authors for this catalogue have contributed meaningful insight to this under-examined subject. In particular I would like to thank Thierry Davila and Sandra Alvarez de Toledo for their collegial discussion over the past couple of years. Sander Gilman and Gwendolyn DuBois Shaw have also gone out of their way to add to this project. Stéphanie Molinard has contributed both to the biographies and to the research for the catalogue and exhibition and I am indebted to her for this help.

Our generous lenders have helped make possible this exhibition, and I would like to thank Harvard University Art Museums; Alvaro Clark and the Associação Cultural "O Mundo de Lygia Clark"; The Museum of Modern Art, New York; Sperone Westwater; Ricardo Resende and the Projeto Leonilson; Tanya Bonakdar; and Ronald Feldman Gallery. The Hohenbüchlers project was made in collaboration with students and assistants of the Institute for Visual Arts, and the Institutes for Science and Technology in the Arts and Architecture, Academy for Visual Arts, Vienna, and I would like to thank them for their work. Above all, however, this project would never have been possible without the contributions of the artists, many of whom have made work specifically for this exhibition. I would like to thank all of them but in particular Tania Bruguera, Cai Guo-Qiang, Bill T. Jones and Gretchen Bender, Irene and Christine Hohenbüchler, David Medalla, Ernesto Neto, and Richard Yarde for their time and consideration in realizing their work at the ICA.

Jessica Morgan, Exhibition Curator

# ESSAYS

## INTRODUCTION

by Jessica Morgan

"ART. IT CURES AFFLICTION"
James Merrill, from *Farewell Performance*

### I

Joseph Beuys and Lygia Clark were born just one year apart, Beuys in Krefeld, Germany, in 1921 (although Beuys later famously reassigned his birthplace to Cleve in accordance with his personal mythology), and Clark in Belo Horizonte, Brazil, in 1920. The similarities between these two artists extend beyond a shared chronology, including, most significantly, their meticulously theorized philosophies of art, both of which entailed a belief in art's therapeutic potential. While this belief was expressed in radically different ways by each artist—indeed Beuys's nigh-shamanistic presence as a "health helper" was diametrically opposed to Clark's insistence on the artist's role not as demiurgic presence but as a mediator of "ritual without myth"—there are many correspondences between their work that suggest more than simply a reflection of the spirit of their time. Viewed side by side, Beuys and Clark complicate and contradict aspects of each other's artistic practice, while representing two interrelated possibilities in late modernist art that continue to resonate in contemporary practice: on the one hand, a highly expressionistic and mystical art form that grounded its spirituality in politics, history, and the everyday; and on the other, a mode that rejected the universalist and utopian in place of an art of the "proposition" to be articulated by the individual in unique psychotherapeutic experiences facilitated by the artist. Uniting both artists was the notion of liberating contemporary life from the sensorially deprived condition of the late twentieth century and the belief that with that reawakening would come a restoration of "health," understood with its broadest implications.

Beuys's and Clark's backgrounds were strikingly different, making any later similarity between their work all the more unexpected. Beuys's youthful ambition to study medicine was interrupted by military service as a radio operator and combat pilot—during which time he reputedly survived an airplane crash in the Crimean steppes with the help of local inhabitants who wrapped him in felt and fat in order to aid his recovery, a story that would bear significantly on his later work. After the war, Beuys witnessed the devastation of postwar Germany and the subsequent reconstruction in the shadow of National Socialism while a student at the Düsseldorf Academy. Clark, meanwhile, born in Minas Gerais, the baroque mining region of Brazil, married at eighteen and also studied somewhat late. In Rio, in the midst of the country's rapid industrialization and a specifically Brazilian modernism, she trained with the landscape designer Roberto Burle-Marx, and then in the 1950s she continued her training in painting with Fernand Léger in Paris—a city she would return to frequently in her life, partly in order to escape Brazil's military dictatorship.

By the mid-1960s, both artists were already fairly well-established figures in their native countries and had clearly identified themselves as avant-garde leaders committed to challenging prescribed notions of artistic practice: Beuys was associated with the Fluxus movement but had already distinguished his work from this group in individual performances and sculpture; and Clark, one of the founding members of the Brazilian Neo-Concrete movement, had subsequently developed her theory of art based on the proposal rather than the finite object. Common to both artists' work was an insistence on the significance of art beyond the narrow confines of an art world or the practice of object making, and a deliberate expansion of the creative process to include the social, psychological, therapeutic, and political. Also by the mid-60s, both Beuys and Clark had articulated concepts of art based on its implicitly beneficial effects—as a structure for promoting healing—and both felt that this therapeutic potential necessitated transference of creativity from the individual artist to the spectator.

Given the extensive literature on Beuys and the increasing attention paid to Clark's output over the last decade, the purpose of a comparative inquiry is not to unearth previously overlooked aspects of their work, but rather to assess the discourse of healing that activates their undertaking and to attempt to identify the manner in which this outlook has influenced subsequent generations. While the differences between the two artists' sensibilities may, in fact, outweigh their similarities, the ambition of this exhibition is to explore the differing proposals of Beuys and Clark, and to understand their concept of a purposeful artistic practice which, despite their numerous followers, stands in opposition to the dominant current mode of art for art's sake. Both this exhibition and the accompanying catalogue seek to ask if art can have a purpose, if it can have an "effect," as the work of both Beuys and Clark suggests. Is contemporary art merely the manufacture of "consolation objects" in an increasingly alienated world, or is there a role for art beyond the recreational? In addition to outlining the fundamental therapeutic concepts of Beuys and Clark, the exhibition presents the work of thirteen contemporary artists whose work could be said to continue this exploration of the transformative effects of art (be they social, political, or medicinal): Gretchen Bender and Bill T. Jones; Tania Bruguera; Cai Guo-Qiang; Felix Gonzalez-Torres; Irene and Christine Hohenbüchler; Wolfgang Laib; Leonilson; David Medalla; Ernesto Neto; Hannah Wilke; and Richard Yarde.

## II

Behind Beuys's and Clark's development of a therapeutic philosophy in their work stand their differing life experience and their native countries' cultural history. In contrast to the prevailing cultural trend in postwar Germany, Beuys deliberately chose to explore a Germanic tradition that was considered tainted by Nazi ideology, precisely in order to rescue the mythology, beliefs, and philosophy that had been co-opted by National Socialism. Beuys's insistence on the significance of place and language—which itself is associated with the soil in German culture—follows a tradition from Johann Gottfried Herder to Martin Heidegger, in which the conception of the work of art grows organically out of the totality of a national spirit. His use of some of the key elements of the ideology of National Socialism—including not only reference to a mythical homeland and a frequent use of pagan and Christian symbols, but in general a politicization of aesthetics—reflects his intention to reclaim and complicate these notions, in a manner that suggests not emulation but retrieval. Beuys viewed the denial of Germanic culture as comparable to the covering of a wound; instead he espoused a tactic of exposure: the showing of wounds (social, physical, and cultural), he proposed, would be the only way to retain proximity with and understanding of the past, allowing for a "healthful" recovery. The remedy, he suggests, is to be found in understanding and even replicating the trauma in order to experience the event as an active participant rather than a passive recipient.

While Beuys's entire oeuvre could be said to be concerned with the notion of health and its attainment, Clark's interest in the therapeutic effects of art developed with her experience of psychoanalysis and her radical transformation of the relationship between artist, object, and spectator from the mid-1960s. Of primary importance in Clark's work is the emphasis on a bodily, interior experience; through her interactive work she proposes a reintegration of the disjointed, contemporary "body of parts" through sensory experience. Her development of this concept was influenced not only by psychoanalytical writing but also by twentieth-century Brazilian cultural thought, including the notion of *antropofagia*, or cannibalism, as proposed by the writer and critic Oswald de Andrade in the 1920s. Andrade's metaphor symbolized the manner in which Brazil "swallowed" various world cultures in order to create its own, not in a hostile fashion but in a spirit of anticolonial defiance. Clark used this cannibalistic metaphor, as critic Guy Brett has described, to develop a radical proposition by which artist, object, and spectator are simultaneously incorporated into one.[1] This theory allowed her to differentiate her work from that of contemporary body artists, whose work, she argued, merely replaced the traditional art object with the artist's body rather than truly addressing the relationship between the body, the intellect, and the lived experience. Paulo Herkenhoff has further suggested that Andrade's idealization of Pindorama—the nineteenth-century literary depiction of primitive Brazil—as a paradise without madness (or a place where the stringent boundaries between health and insanity are dissolved) influenced Clark's development of an alternative therapy in reaction to the disparity that she observed between the treatment of the physical and the psychological.[2]

Implicit in both Beuys's and Clark's culturally and contextually informed philosophies is the suggestion of a primary state of being or "origin" that needs to be accessed in order for recovery to occur. In Beuys's work, this original state is closely associated with elemental forces—represented in his work by animals, minerals, and vegetables and the cultural or mythical origins of society—that will re-energize contemporary man, bridging the gap between alienated urban life and some sort of natural condition. Clark's concept of a "primary" state implies a mind-body totality in which no one sense is given priority and the subject is able to overcome the opposed, physical and psychic states of inside/outside. Clark's proposition extends beyond a mere sensualism and points toward a potent social goal in a spirit akin to Rousseau. While Beuys's work suggests a kind of nostalgia for an elemental condition, Clark does not mourn this lost state, which she sees as irretrievable, but like Beuys, she strives for the sensory completeness depleted by contemporary everyday life—both artists, in fact, could be said to attempt a healing of modern culture. Crucially, for both Beuys and Clark, it is through the spectator's transformation, from passive receiver to active participant, that such a restoration or reconnection to an "origin" might take place.

Much of Beuys's work utilizes materials or actions emblematic of the primary forces he identified, which the artist then channeled for their therapeutic or energy-giving properties. *Coyote: I Like America and America Likes Me*, Beuys's infamous performance in New York City in 1974, is perhaps the best-known event that embodied such an attempt at communication and healing. For this relatively late performance, Beuys arrived at Kennedy Airport and was transported by a siren-blaring ambulance to Galerie René Block where the event, and by suggestion some kind of healing, were to take place. Placed together in a caged room over a period of three days, Beuys and a coyote gradually became familiar with each other's presence, and the initially frantic, pacing animal relaxed. For Beuys the coyote had metaphorical force as a sign not only of the gap between our natural state and our urban present, but as an American Indian symbol of harmony, and, by extension, a reference to the decimated state of contemporary Indian life in America. Wrapped in his signature felt and clutching a staff, Beuys's highly controlled action—the event was initially delayed as he disapproved of the metal caging supplied by the gallery—typified his role as shaman/mediator and acted as a demonstration of his central role in this direction of natural forces. The spatial division of the cage clearly delineated the division between artist and spectator: the audience's participation depended on a projected belief in the initiation-like ceremony that Beuys had constructed with the coyote, whereby Beuys the shaman, communicating with the wild animal, mediated or transformed the wordless dialogue into a healing process for others.

Such a performance is unthinkable in Clark's work, where her own presence, although intrinsic to much of her work, is reduced to that of activator working in tandem with object and spectator, both of which are similarly transformed from their normative states. Although the search for the attainment, through therapeutic practice, of some primary state of being was only clearly articulated with her use of the *Objetos relacionais* (Relational Objects) from the mid-1970s, her earlier works logically follow a trajectory to this point. From the simple objects made to be manipulated that form the series *Nostalgia del cuerpo* (Nostalgia of the Body)—for example *Respire comigo* (Breathe with Me), a rubber tube that when repeatedly stretched emulates the sound of breathing—to the series *La casa es el cuerpo* (The House Is the Body)—which included the *Máscaras sensoriais*, cloth masks fitted with different devices to transform hearing, vision, and sense of smell—and the "communal propositions" of *Fantasmática del cuer-*

*po* (The Phantasmagoria of the Body)—which included *Baba antropofágica*, for which a group of participants with reels of cotton in their mouths slowly draw out the thread in order to cover the body of another, prostrate participant—Clark's work is suggestive of a reconnection to the senses and thereby to some preverbal form of communication. All the while, the artist, if present at all, remains merely the facilitator of transformation rather than a healer.

While the concept of accessing some primal state that was by implication a more "truthful" expression was not new to their art—artists associated with surrealism had made use of an "automatic" art that emerged from an unconscious state of being (a strategy that was transformed by *tachisme, art informel,* and early work by American abstract expressionists), and *art brut* had proposed a return to a supposedly intuitive practice—Beuys's and Clark's significant departure was in developing an art form that focused not on the transformation of the artist but of the spectator. Theirs was not an art of alienated expression but rather an attempt to bridge the perceived gap between individuals and their lived experience. Among their various strategies devised to break the normative relationship between artist or object and viewer, Beuys and Clark each experimented with different forms of sensual interaction. Both artists' work reflects a movement away from a perceived dependence on the visual in art, suggesting that the purely visual experience can be overanalytical or "cold" as opposed to the intuitive response of the other senses. Reawakening the sensory capacities of their audience through the activation of the other senses frequently takes the form of tactile, kinetic, olfactory, or audio components in their work. Moreover, both artists produced objects or incorporated materials that have a direct relationship to the body—Clark sometimes mimicking the appearance or function of bodily organs in her objects and Beuys referencing bodily substances. While Clark literally encouraged her spectators to manipulate objects or experience a deprivation or deception of sight in order to heighten other senses, Beuys conveyed such experience symbolically by the presence of evocative and redolent materials such as honey, felt, and fat.

Clearly both artists were not alone in the 1960s and 70s in their use of participation in their work. In Latin America many other artists, including Clark's sometime collaborator and close friend Hélio Oiticica, as well as Lygia Pape, Lea Lublin, and Marta Minujin, were making environments, objects, and installations that involved audience participation, and in Europe and North America, in addition to the artists associated with the Fluxus movement, artists such as Vito Acconci, Franz Erhard Walther, and Bruce Nauman were similarly producing work that required spectator activation. Undoubtedly Beuys's and Clark's work was affected by the political consciousness of the 60s and the accompanying emphasis on the importance of a communal and demonstrative involvement in social and political events, a commitment that was directly reflected in much contemporary art production at that time. What sets their work apart, however, is the central place given to the concept of transformation through participation, a belief largely absent in the work of others of their generation whose use of the collaborative or participatory is suggestive of a more generalized conception of the necessity for communal activity, either as a guarantee of the social relevance of the work or as a means to extend the individual physical or psychological experience of the artist to the group.

With Beuys and Clark, the role of the spectator/participant is theorized to a remarkable degree, and the consequent ambitions for this new relationship between artist and audience are manifestly increased. Beuys's proposal was summed up in his oft-misinterpreted statement that "every man is an artist," whereby he suggested that what he referred to as "social sculpture" called for a change in the public as great as that undertaken by the artist and artwork, and that the audience must actively participate in this change in order for the holistic, humane potential of the work to emerge. Beuys's expanded interpretation of sculpture, which included teaching, cognition, exchange, and protest, transformed the normative process of artistic communication between individuals into a more democratic conception of audience participation. For Clark, though it was limited to individuals rather than the mass, participation remained the cornerstone of her philosophy. In 1983, five years before her death, her manifesto still reflected this:

Participation totally transforms the meaning of art as we have understood it until now. Because:

We reject the representative space and the work as a passive contemplation;

we reject all myth exterior to man;

we reject the work of art itself and attach more importance to the act of carrying out the proposition;

we reject duration as a method of expression.

We propose the very time of the act as a field of experience. In a world in which man has become estranged as to his work, we incite him, through the experience, to become aware of the alienation in which he lives.[3]

Clark thus viewed the experience of participation in her work not as a (subsequent) reflection of a reality—either utopian or present—but as what she referred to as an (anticipatory) "preparation for life.

The objects and installations of Beuys and Clark share an incompleteness, lack of definition, or partial, unfinished quality that for both artists acted as stimulant for the spectator/participant, whose role was to complete or activate the work either through interaction or projection. This quality in particular was necessary for both artists, who wished their work to hover somewhere between the transitory and the eternal, evading the confines of a merely local communication. Their proposals or actions were therefore at once ephemeral in their substance and radically infinite in their proposition, which was nothing short of social change. Although aesthetically Beuys and Clark may appear at odds, their work is characterized by the use of materials that were, particularly at their time of use, considered unworthy of art—for Beuys these were almost always natural materials, whereas Clark typically utilized readily available found objects such as plastic bags, rubber tubing, string netting, shells, and stones. The transformation that Beuys's work undergoes as a result of climate, age, and natural decay is deliberate, and points to the complexity of the metaphorical and literal significance of his chosen materials. Beuys most frequently employed fat, felt, copper, and iron (which symbolically represent storage, insulation, conduction, mass, and weight), and for the artist the changeable nature of fat, in particular, which when heated melts and becomes gaseous and when cold contracts into a solid, was comparable to the creative and lived experience: precarious and reversible. Clark's choice of common materials was in part directed by their sensory significance but was also a reflection of her determination not to reify the object. Significantly, she did not generally use natural materials—perhaps in order to avoid the generative or maternal associations that are inevitably made when a woman artist employs organic matter, but more likely as she felt that no specific material should be seen as intrinsically significant or "life-giving." The transformative potential of the object for Clark is brought about through interaction, not association.

This conflicting approach to materials points to Beuys's and Clark's fundamentally incompatible attitude toward the object. For Clark, from the time that she began the series *Nostalgia del cuerpo*, the object was merely a cipher or container that had no meaning per se until activated by interaction. Similarly, the physical body for Clark had architectural or structural properties as a container but was only made significant through experiential activation. In contrast, Beuys's work is characterized by a reification of the body and its substance, and all events in his work, however ephemeral or momentary, are memorialized in objects understood to contain symbolic reference. Although Clark never relinquished the object in her practice, she intrinsically distrusted the museum sphere and the normative relations it imposed on the audience/art object/artist triumvirate. Her objects, such as those made for *Nostalgia del cuerpo* but also the earlier metal *Bichos*, or animals, were made to be handled or manipulated and thus contradicted museum strictures to preserve and protect and thus not to touch. The events that formed the series *Fantasmática del cuerpo* were, moreover, intended not for an audience but rather for a select group of participants, all of whom contributed to, and benefited from, the experience. All that remains of *Baba antropofágica*, for example, are the odd still photograph and the participants' accounts of the process of collectively disgorging the thread from their mouths or the memory of the prostrate figure engorged in this process. Beuys's performances, in contrast, were carefully orchestrated affairs that took place almost exclusively in museum, gallery, or official settings and were carefully documented through still images and film, approved by the artist, as well as unique objects or editions related to the event. This remained the case even once his work had developed primarily into pedagogical or political events, which were similarly recorded photographically or through the preservation of material remnants. This significance of the object for Beuys, however, did not contradict his corresponding attempt to subvert its exchange value in cultural economics. Part of Beuys's interest in producing multiples, for example, or in signing anything that was presented to him, was aimed at confusing the notions of scarcity and originality that occupy and inflate the art market.

Beuys's and Clark's common desire to establish an artistic practice that brought about therapeutic transmogrification, moreover, developed almost in reverse. While Beuys began as an artist producing objects and installations that called for an intimate and personal reading, his later projects involved such mass events as public lectures, the founding of political parties, and the development of new pedagogical forms. Clark, in contrast, experimented first with group activities on an increasingly large scale, but ultimately turned to an individual practice with one subject/patient interacting with her *Objetos relacionais*. While Beuys's objective was increasingly to effect social change on a scale that such transformation demands, Clark's aim, even in the collaborative events, was to bring about individual, psychological healing, albeit with the ultimate aim of transforming society. Beuys literally attempted to change the structures that governed the creative and social realms, whereas Clark attempted to transform the role of the artist and challenge the hierarchy of creative control. It is tempting to consider, in light of these two opposing strategies, that there is also a gender-driven difference in evidence. Beuys, famously criticized for the authorial centrality and shaman-like significance in his own work, stands in stark contrast to Clark's increasingly transparent and profoundly democratic artistic role: performance and display as opposed to mediation and negation.

## III

While Beuys and Clark worked in the aftermath of the Second World War, a trauma that for Beuys in particular was the defining event in his work, the thirteen contemporary artists selected for this exhibition have developed in a relatively peaceful time. Their work, however, is similarly marked by contemporary events—from the advent of new diseases such as AIDS and the increasingly chemical and clinical treatment of illness that coincided with the rapid development of the pharmaceutical industry, to the global expansion of Western commodity culture, its validation of youth and "health," and the concomitant banishment of age and illness from popular and commercial space. The state of sensory deprivation deplored by Beuys and Clark has been efficaciously systematized throughout daily life to an extent no doubt unimaginable to either artist, from the sterile space of car culture to the growth of digital "communication." Each of the artists in the exhibition has struggled with these developments, and many have addressed directly the legacy of Beuys and/or Clark. While proposing a concept of an efficacious art practice in the face of the self-referential nature of the majority of artistic practices in the past decades, many of the artists have developed participatory artworks that address the ongoing attempt to challenge the normative relationship between artist, object, and spectator.

Although the majority of artists included in *Pulse* represent generations subsequent to Beuys and Clark, Philippine-born David Medalla's early performances, installations, and sculpture were conceived simultaneous to Beuys's and Clark's activities in the 1960s, and he continues to develop many of their shared concerns from that time. Medalla's *A Stitch in Time* consists of a suspended construction of rope, cotton reels, and sheets of fabric on which visitors are invited to embroider or write with the needles and thread provided. Like Oiticica and Clark, Medalla interpretes such audience participation more profoundly in terms of the "life experience" of the individual and social body. Politically charged, *A Stitch in Time* enigmatically suspends the activity of stitching somewhere between labor and leisure, between the present moment and what the artist calls "genetic memory."

Many of the artists included in the exhibition arrived at their interest in the relationship between art and healing through their own experience of illness or loss, comparable to the impact of war and trauma on Beuys, or the transformative experience of psychoanalysis for Clark. Their production has in addition been influenced by a feminist art practice of the 1970s that argued for a relevance, both theoretical and political, that could be extrapolated from the personal experience. The work of Leonilson and Hannah Wilke tragically documents their gradual decline and death due respectively to AIDS and cancer. After Brazilian-born Leonilson's illness forced him to give up painting, he concentrated on stitching panels and embroidering pieces of fabric with personally symbolic words and images. The diary-like activity documented the artist's deteriorating health and impending death. Several of the works were created as gifts for friends, occasionally made from cloth they had given him, sometimes from pieces of his own clothing. Despite their ephemerality and small scale, the embroidered works crystallize many of the themes that had appeared throughout Leonilson's work: abandonment, desire, loss, and illness. Wilke established her presence as a politically active performance artist in the 1970s, only to revisit her early work and its use of her own striking physical presence in a series that documented her worsening health. Attempting to make sense of death, a subject she had previously explored in a series of works documenting her mother's similar deterioration from cancer, Wilke navigates the complex issues of beauty and the gaze, identity and self in the face of her own drastic transformation.

The work of Felix Gonzalez-Torres and Richard Yarde is similarly informed by their own experience of sickness. *Untitled (Placebo),* a candy spill by Gonzalez-Torres, serves as a reminder of how the artist's constantly renewable and emphatic art proffers the promise of healing and the hope of regeneration while simultaneously questioning the authority of the medical and legal professions. The pile of silver-wrapped candy lies enticingly on the gallery floor, inviting a participation that begs the descriptive cliché "bitter sweet." While the offer is genuine, the title points to the political war that raged in the 90s over access and funding for the treatment and research of HIV and AIDS. Yarde similarly suffered a catastrophic illness—complete kidney failure that left him incapacitated with stroke-like symptoms in 1991. With impaired movement and loss of speech, Yarde stopped making art for more than a year. After a self-described "spiritual awakening" he slowly returned to painting, although he has stated that his hands felt stiff and foreign. Palms and hands—wooden mannequin hands—dominate the works from the first stages of his recovery, mirroring his visual investigations into the primacy of a belief in the healing powers of touch in the evolution of religious thought. Later works include dots and markers derived from the deluge of X-rays and medical data physicians were using to map his body, utilized by Yarde to mediate the medical investigation of his own inner bodyscape.

The significance of audience participation or action is fundamental to many of the works by Cai Guo-Qiang that merge the sensorial tactility of Clark's work and the holistic philosophy of Beuys with the artist's own Eastern perspective. *A cure when ill, a supplement when healthy* is an interactive installation that incorporates principles from acupuncture, foot reflexology, and traditional Chinese medicine. On the floor of the gallery is a path made of pebbles of different sizes and shapes, which visitors can walk on after removing their shoes. On the wall next to the path are drawings explaining the theories of reflexology, which viewers can read as they traverse the course, at the end of which is a vending machine filled with bottled herbal cures. One can insert money into the machine, choose one of the five cures for a particular ailment, and buy a tonic. Viewers thus perform a kind of self-induced reflexology treatment and have the opportunity to take an herbal medicine.

Ernesto Neto is one of the few Brazilian artists of his generation who have seriously taken up some of the fundamental issues raised by Clark's work. His *Ovaloids* are oval structures about one meter in height filled with Styrofoam pellets; they sit directly on the ground. The *Ovaloids* have orifices into which the visitor can insert a hand (or even an arm) and touch (through the protective Lycra membrane) the thousands of little balls that make up the internal organs of the work. Echoing the objects that Clark produced both for assisted therapeutic practice and for individual playful use, these *Ovaloids* evoke a sensual, humorous, and experimental approach to the body.

The works of Cuban artist Tania Bruguera and Austrian sisters Irene and Christine Hohenbüchler approach this question of participation from the radical perspective of Clark, transferring the act of making to the audience/participant. Bruguera's performance, installation, and video work is made in response to a political and cultural environment, whether it be the relationship between art and power in Cuba, emigration, memory, or, more recently, silence, guilt, and responsibility. Ritual, obsessive repetition for cathartic purposes and the fallacy of utopian proposals are all part of the structure of her work. Bruguera's series *Behavior Art: Translations* attempts to extend her performance work by transferring the role of performer or communicator to an untrained subject. In various cities including London, Delhi, and Lima, Bruguera has worked with a non-artist to perform one of her works. Bruguera provides the subject with the information on the theme or issue of the performance and asks the subject to interpret these concerns from his or her own perspective. In each city, the subject chosen to perform is from a minority group—in Delhi for example the performer was a Muslim living in Hindu India, and in London Bruguera worked with a Scot who had visited the English capital only once before. The Hohenbüchlers work with institutionalized groups of various kinds, in particular those with learning difficulties, but also with prisoners and psychiatric patients. Although theirs is a creative process based on intersubjective communication, the sisters do not function as therapists. Their strategy, which they call *Multiple Autorenschaft* (Multiple Authorship), offers a framework that can be filled with meaning by patients as collaborative partners. Collaboration with a group of handicapped children in Copenhagen, for example, focused on the communal dining table as the setting for their project. The Hohenbüchlers alternately organized cooking and art-making projects that resulted in finished artworks and testimony to their challenge of institutional form and social practice.

Ritual was central to both Beuys's and Clark's artistic production, and the therapeutic potential of ritualistic behavior is investigated in a number of works in the exhibition. Wolfgang Laib's work revolves around the cycles of nature and nature's relationship to beauty, faith, ritual, and healing. The patient activity of gathering pollen and beeswax is central to the production of many of his sculptures and installations. Laib's *Rice Bowls*, a minimal line of simple convex bronze receptacles, hold ingredients symbolic of sustenance, growth, and proliferation: rice and pollen. Dance has long been concerned with the performance of rituals—both mundane and sacred—and the exhibition includes Bill T. Jones's collaborative dance project *Still/Here*. The performance, which premiered in Lyons, France, in 1994, was the result of eleven workshops with survivors of life-threatening illnesses. In the US it was accused in some quarters of glorifying "victimhood"—vocalizing the reactionary response to much of the personal narrative-based art that had proliferated in the late 80s and early 90s. Though painfully direct in its use of testaments to individuals' suffering, the choreography ultimately works to realize and even overcome the disjunction experienced in sickness between the physical, the mental, and the sensory. *Still/Here* examines issues of creativity, humanity, and the reality of inhabiting the same body as death. The film *Still/Here* was codirected by Jones and multimedia artist Gretchen Bender and documents the creation of the dance piece by the same name.

## IV

Beuys and Clark generated remarkably few direct imitators. Beuys's influence as a pedagogue was philosophical and political but not necessarily aesthetic, such that some of his most famous pupils—such as Blinky Palermo and Imi Knoebel—were not sculptors or performance artists but painters. Given the central, demiurgic presence of the artist in his work, it would of course be hard to imitate his practice, but the concept of a healing art is one that perhaps faded in Germany alongside the memory of the Second World War. Similarly, at the time of Clark's death, her individual therapeutic practice that utilized the *Objetos rela-*

*cionais* had attracted very few collaborators, and it has taken a few generations for her proposals to be thoroughly reconsidered in a contemporary Brazilian context. The thirteen artists above, therefore, have not emerged from a coherent development of a therapeutically inclined art practice. Indeed, as mentioned at the outset, such an apparently purposeful type of art making is widely regarded with suspicion. Art, it is generally felt, unlike our many other activities in life, should remain free of any direct purpose, and the suggestion of its efficaciousness is taken as dangerously close to irrational, fetishistic behavior. This lingering irrational hope, however, and the desire for a belief in art as an experience directly related to but substantively different from our daily activities, is precisely what activates even the most meticulously theorized work such as that of Beuys and Clark. Whether or not we expect some transformative effect to take place, it is this kernel of hope—that our knowledge of the world will be enhanced by the experience of art—that continues to engage us whether or not the work is manifestly intended to heal us.

1 Guy Brett in *Lygia Clark* (Barcelona: Fundació Antoni Tàpies, 1998), p. 24.
2 Paulo Herkenhoff in ibid., p. 47.
3 Lygia Clark, "We Reject," in ibid., p. 211.

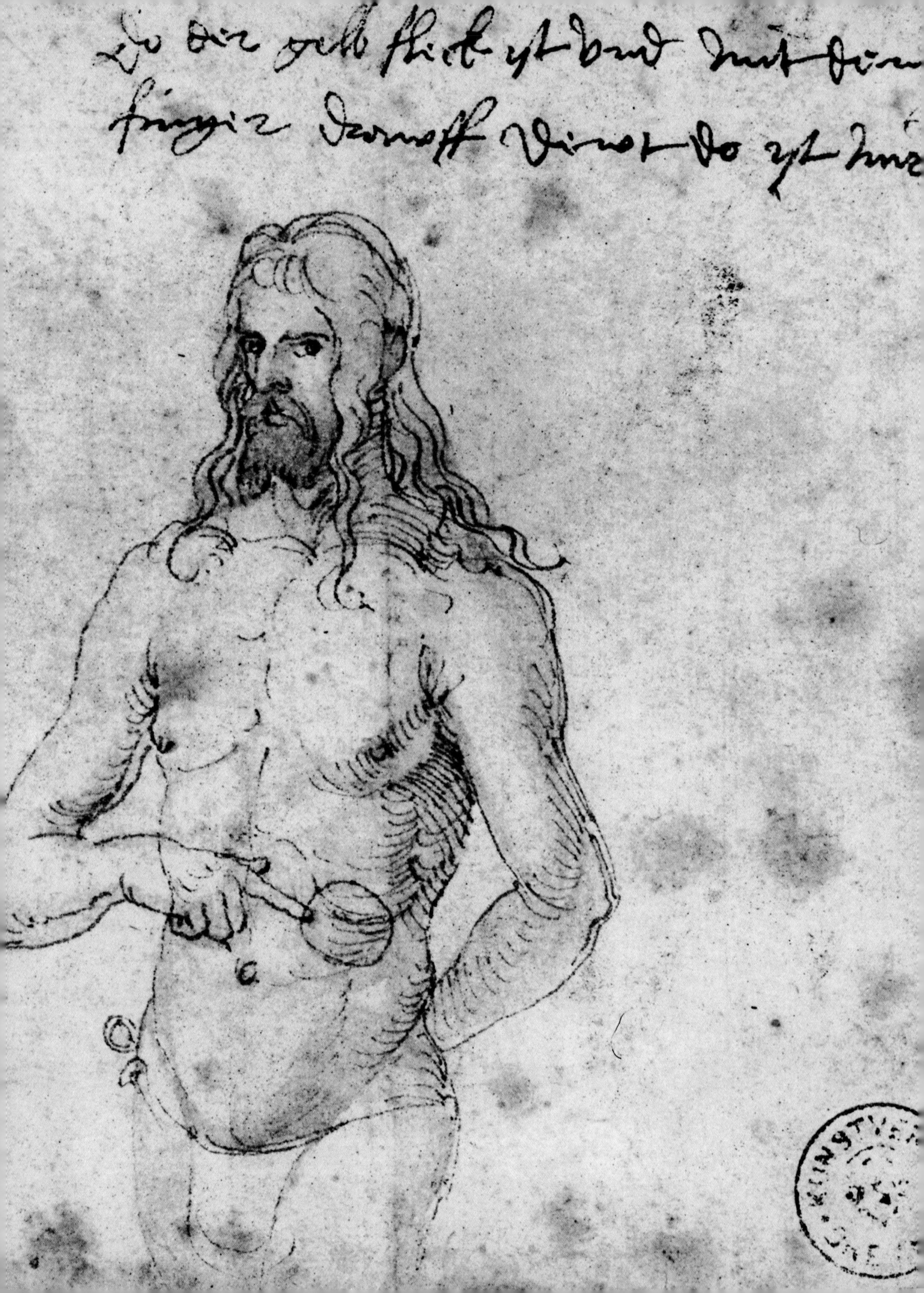

## THE REMEDY IN THE AFFLICTION: JOSEPH BEUYS

by Thierry Davila

"How did you learn your profession?"
"I started by being sick."

Dialogue between anthropologist Victor Turner and a Ndembu medicine man.[1]

"I would say the following: what I do can be directly related to medicine."

Joseph Beuys[2]

The man is wearing only a loincloth, held by a thin string around his waist and hiding his genitals. His face, his long hair, and his beard are reminiscent of Jesus. One of his hands is hidden behind his massive torso. With the index finger of his other hand, the right, he points to an area on the left side of his body, the side he is also staring at, as if to underscore visually what the hand is trying to indicate. Above the figure (in this wash drawing) is a German sentence that can be read as a caption: "The yellow spot I am pointing at is where it hurts." A circle marks the place where pain has manifested itself on the artist's flesh. But what is this illness that has become the material—the raw material—for a work of art? What suffering is powerful enough, *great* enough, to warrant such *exhibition*? And what is doing the work here? The drawing and, beyond it, the sovereign hand that drew it? The illness working on the body itself to constitute a wound, shaping the material and thus leading an almost naked man wracked by pain to expose himself, to make a spectacle of himself? Or both together, so inextricably intertwined as to bring together on a sheet of paper illness and art, illness *as* art?

Completed in 1512 or 1513, this self-portrait by Albrecht Dürer in the guise of suffering patient was "apparently done for the purpose of consulting a physician" and allegedly indicates the locus of the pain as the spleen, "supposed to be the source of black bile, the cause of melancholy."[3] On this view, it is similar to the small statues of jade and ivory that the Chinese use to show a caregiver where a pain is located without having to undress.[4] More importantly, this image, in which Dürer established a physical resemblance between himself and Christ, led to a conflation of the *personal value* of suffering with its *expository value*, of the inner disarray due to illness and its ravages with their transformation into a spectacle, their presentation as an offering to all mankind. In the Munich self-portrait of 1500, Dürer used this similarity of appearance with the Redeemer and Son of God to turn his face and person into an analogue of the Christ figure.[5] In 1503, it was a very Christ-like wound, similar to the wounds caused by one or more lances, that figured in a new self-portrait of the artist, again evoking a comparison between the history of a suffering mortal and the history of a god. Later, in 1522, Dürer made an engraving of a man in pain in which the figure of Christ again appears with the artist's own features: this image shows a dying man holding the instruments of his Passion (rods and a whip). Dürer's *Self-Portrait as a Sick Man* is thus also intended to establish an analogy between

Albrecht Dürer,
*Self Portrait as a Sick Man, 1512–1513.*
Collection of
Kunsthalle Bremen

Dürer's pain (with its associated wounds) and the Passion of God made flesh.[6] Here the traumatic power of pain secretly reinforces its expository power; the lethal, destructive force of suffering surreptitiously enhances its demonstrative potential. In a work dating from 1510, Dürer depicted Christ as a man in pain pointing to a wound on the right side of his naked body, dramatizing his final Passion. Two years later, the Munich self-portrait would take up the same motif in a more intimate and melancholic vein, yet without neglecting its demonstrative aspect, its intention as spectacle.[7]

The work of Joseph Beuys resonates deeply with that of Dürer in at least two respects: on the theme of the wound[8] and its expository value as well as the theme of the sick man, both fundamental motifs in a body of work in which they recur again and again. These motifs mark the inauguration of that work, the beginning. In 1964, the artist prepared his *Curriculum vita—Curriculum operae* for the catalog of the Festival of Aix-la-Chapelle, and he would continue to add to it until 1969 (at which time he characterized his participation in the festival as an "art pill"). His birth in Clèves (actually Krefeld) in 1921 is there described as the "exhibition of a wound closed with a bandage."[9] All of his work from that point on would deal with suffering, trauma, and everything they imply (treatment, cure). Thus in 1974, for the action *Coyote: I Like America and America Likes Me* mounted for the inauguration of the René Block Gallery in New York, Beuys arrived at Kennedy Airport completely wrapped in felt and lying on a stretcher, and from there he was transported to the gallery in an ambulance with siren blaring. After spending three days there with a coyote, he returned, once again as a patient, to the airport. That same year he began work on *Show Your Wound*, which was exhibited for the first time in Munich in 1976. The work includes two racks from a morgue, and its title and motif establish a profound resonance with Dürer's portrait of himself as a sick man.[10] In 1985, in delivering a *Speech on My Country*, the artist made a statement that sounds like a methodological discovery about his own work: "Once again, I seem to want to begin with a wound."[11] Apart from these well-known and frequently analyzed examples, medical items (such as bandages, gauze, flasks, test tubes, dressings, prostheses, and so on) can be found in many of the artist's works, along with a symbol of medicine, the red cross (the emblem of an international organization established in 1863 to care for the victims of war, whose purpose today is to bring aid wherever it is needed in the world). These works include *Show Your Wound, Skin, Homogeneous Infiltration for Grand Piano,* etc. Wounds and diseases are depicted as *afflictions*, as *historical disturbances*, in two senses: they afflict individuals with trauma and suffering (Beuys's war wounds and personal crises) before being overcome by a person blessed with healing powers, and they afflict not only German society, traumatized by World War II, but also Western man and Western society in general (the West is portrayed as the victim of a mistaken conception of production and creativity, which it is the artist's mission to heal).[12]

This is where the figure of Christ comes in, as one who is capable of healing humanity because he suffered with it and for it. Beuys uses this image in a variety of ways (the red cross can also become the cross of the crucifixion); it is another motif that figures abundantly in his work. For instance, in 1962 the artist created a sculpture called *Crucifixion* out of discarded materials, the central portion of which consists of a piece of wood topped with a cross painted on a sheet of newsprint. In 1964, in the course of a complex action carried out in Aix-la-Chapelle, *Kukei/akopee-Non/Croix brune/Coins de graisse/Coins de graisse modèles*, which evoked Germany's Nazi past, he was punched in the face by a student. Beuys, his nose bloodied, reacted by imitating the Nazi salute and brandishing in his left hand a crucifix mounted on a base. In 1971, on an image of Jesus, he wrote in German *The Inventor of the Steam Engine*, which was the title of the work. Then he repeated this act on an identical image, but this time with the title *Inventor of the Third Law of Thermodynamics*. That same year he performed another action, entitled *Celtic* +~~, in which he imitated Christ by washing the feet of seven individuals. These few examples, which are well known, show how systematically the figure and symbolism of Christ were enlisted to enhance the person and work of the artist.

For Beuys, the reference to the cross (as the representative sign of our civilization, which he associates with the crystalline principle and with the principle of chaotic order)[13] and to Christ leads to a certain way of looking at the world: "You have to think of things both horizontally and vertically [Beuys draws a cross]. Christ was attached to this thing."[14] But it is also a way of combining suffering and remission so that they become inseparable: Jesus—about whom the most important things, in the artist's eyes, are the recurrent episodes[15] of healing that mark his history—is the man who showed his wounds to all in order to save mankind, and the cross is equally a symbol of death and of healing. By invoking and representing the acts and symbols of Jesus, Beuys reactivates the suffering-healing polarity, which can also be seen in the person of the shaman.

In fact, the medicine man, continuing the figure of Christ in this respect, can represent or incarnate the possibility of healing only because he himself has suffered the intense effects of an illness or radical personal crisis, only because he passed through death so as to remain, more than anyone else, alive. This "disease-vocation"[16] or "initiatory disease"[17] leads him to assume the role of healer by way of death and resurrection, of resolution of suffering through experimentation, because "the medicine man is above all one who has himself recovered from illness, who has healed himself."[18] And "if [shamans] are themselves healed and know how to heal others, one reason for this is that they understand the mechanism, or better still, the theory, of disease."[19] Beuys has often identified with the shaman in his work, particularly in *Coyote: I Like America and America Likes Me*, in which the artist, pretending to be a patient, attempts conversation with a coyote, like a shaman who tries to talk to an animal. The purpose of this communication is to attain a utopian state of remission from all ills.[20] Beuys, in shaping his own biography, has emphasized various initiation rites that make him look something like a shaman. He contrasts afflictions with remedies, injuries with appropriate treatments. The medicine man embodies this double polarity through his ability to overcome his own troubles in order to cope with the disorders of others and defend life and health against afflictions of all kinds.[21] Thus the episode with the Tartars, in which Beuys is supposedly treated (with fat and felt) by nomadic tribesmen after his fighter plane is shot down over the steppes, becomes a kind of "limit experience" that legitimates his work as a form of therapy. Whether or not this actually happened does not matter: traditional shamans, before they can claim the power to heal, must say that they have undergone trials of this kind whether or not they have actually been sick.[22] The point is that episodes of this kind have a structural function within a *medical system*. Beuys says that the trial he allegedly endured forced him to survive "where no one would normally have survived"[23] and thus to experience nothingness in such a way as to transform its negative principle into a vital dynamic and himself into a kind of medicine man possessing "knowledge of death."[24] Once again we see the impulse to establish a dialectical relation between the dead and the living, disease and its remedy, for therapeutic purposes: "In the end, the principal function of the shaman always turns out to be healing, no matter how diverse the facts and explanations and no matter how the therapist and his activities are characterized: as magical, psychological, fraudulent, or religious."[25]

The same polarity is active in the motif of the wound, the inaugural form of Beuys's work: whether exhibited in the form of a dressing glued to paper or extended in space to fill an entire room (*Show Your Wound*), it represents a true floating object that can be both an exhibition of suffering and an indication of a healing process. Nevertheless, disease and trauma enjoy theoretical as well as plastic preeminence. Beuys's work-life, in his sculpted biography, begins with the exhibition of a wound closed with a bandage, and this is not simply an iconographic motif but a true methodological requirement: one must begin with a wound, that is, with knowledge of pain.[26] This approach to method takes a tack opposite to that of much of classical aesthetics, and to Winckelmann's aesthetics in particular, in which illness is excluded from the sphere of artistic representation. Dedicated to imitation of the Ancients in order to justify its own assertion of inimitability, art, according to Winckelmann, must accept the Greek criteria of beauty and the bodies it produces—bodies invariably devoid of physical marks and signs of illness.[27] "The illnesses that destroy so many beauties and disfigure the most perfect bodies were still unknown to the Greeks. ... Nor did venereal diseases or rickets work their ravages on the natural beauty of the Greeks. As a general rule, anything taught or inspired by nature and art susceptible of contributing to the flourishing, preservation, development, and embellishment of the body from birth to maturity was put to use by the ancient Greeks for the purpose of enhancing physical beauty, so that we may say that in all likelihood their physical beauty was superior to ours."[28] In such a historical and theoretical framework, there is no room at all in art for disease and suffering portrayed as such. By making disease and suffering the source of his own sculpture and drawing, Beuys thus declared from the outset that the aesthetic context in which he was working owed nothing at all to the classical canon.

Yet the choice of the wound as working method also has a certain *medical* rationale.[29] Beuys, who in biographical notices composed in 1961 mentioned Nietzsche among his "literary impressions" of the war years,[30] probably knew that disease and health played an important role in Nietzsche's philosophy, and he was probably familiar with the law that inextricably links the two. In fact, Nietzsche looked upon morbid states as a way of shedding light on those organic states we call "normal." Disease teaches us to see what health is: "What is valuable in all morbid conditions is that they put normal states under a microscope, giving us a glimpse of what is normally difficult to see."[31] In support of this assertion, the philosopher quoted a passage from Claude Bernard's *Lectures on Animal Heat*: "Health and sickness are not two essentially different modes, as ancient physicians may have believed and as some practitioners still believe today. One must guard against treating them as two distinct principles, two entities that vie for possession of the living organism and use it as the theater of their struggles. This is old-fashioned medicine. In reality, there are only differences of degree between the two manners: exaggeration, disproportion, and disharmony in normal phenomena constitute the diseased state."[32] The difference between a sick organ and an organ essential to health is merely qualitative, and it reveals the distance that separates sickness from well-being, just as madness forces us to reflect on the nature of reason, to listen to reason.[33] Sickness is therefore a *point of view* from which to look at health, a way of evaluating it,[34] and to experience suffering or injury is a way of discovering the lines of force of a true medicine or at any rate a true therapy, because only through suffering and injury do we discovery the nature of life. Enduring pain, without which understanding of the living is impossible, is the price that the philosopher of the future, who is both a physiologist and an artist, must pay in order to become a "physician to civilization."[35]

Beuys, who is simultaneously artist, Christ, and shaman, dreams of a global medicine addressed to all humanity that would involve, first and foremost, comprehension of pain, which is alone capable of pointing the way to authentic survival. It follows from this that sickness and trauma impose methodological requirements, a way of working on the social, of sculpting the social: if Beuys's actions are a way of analyzing sculpture,[36] the exhibition of suffering and illness are a way of analyzing the state of the patient and of society, of evaluating their vitality or their ailments and developing treatments for them. Each time the artist exhibits a wound, he simultaneously indicates not only a certain *deviation from health* but also a quantity of affliction useful for constituting or elaborating part of the needed remedy.[37] In this respect, he is also in the line of Novalis, for whom death and sickness are man's best opportunities for learning how to heal and save himself: "How many ways are there to *kill*? Methods of killing and of making people sick necessarily shed much light on ways of giving life and healing."[38] This leads to the idea that "illnesses are surely an object *of the highest importance for humanity*,"[39] an object capable not only of teaching us many things about our own condition but also of healing us by treating the destructive effects of disease through the affliction itself. Novalis set forth the principle of this effective medicine: "Pursue the idea of healing illnesses with illnesses."[40] For Beuys, the idea of a "remedy in the affliction" becomes the very principle of therapy itself.[41]

To begin with, it defines the ambivalence or oscillation of the signs and figures that structure his entire oeuvre (the cross, the Christ figure, the wound, the shaman). Each of these is both a harbinger of death and a sign of life, a token of affliction or suffering and an indicator or means of healing. These floating objects become involved in a dialectic, and they also embody a therapeutic resource, a possible treatment for a range of afflictions endured by individual bodies as well as the social body, afflictions brought on by historical change and supposedly capable of indicating or signaling (by what process remains to be seen) a subversion of death by death itself, a defeat of illness by mobilizing the suffering it imposes on the patient against it. *Show Your Wound* crystallizes this dialectic in a particularly acute manner. Each of the objects in the piece is doubled: there are two forks affixed to two slabs of slate on which two incomplete circles are drawn; there are also two stretchers, two blackboards, two tools for stripping the bark from trees, each marked with a cross, two boxes made of galvanized sheet metal with glass windows in them, two test tubes, two zinc pans filled with grease, two thermometers, two jars sealed with cotton, two copies of the newspaper *Lotta continua*, two pieces of tattered fabric wound around the foot of each of the forks, a blackbird skull at the bottom of one test tube and another at the top of the other test tube, both tubes being sealed with cotton. Set on the grease in the two open pans, two parallel test tubes represent movement in opposite directions: the bird's skull in one is a kind of *caput mortuum*, while that in the other seems ready to leap from its container or to be expelled from it. This slight displacement of a form that symbolizes death, this modest shift or minimal variation, is basically just a spatially delimited sign of a potentially more general displacement of each of the objects in the piece toward a direction, function, space of action, or inscription opposite to the one it occupies at any given point in time (for instance: a morgue rack can become a treatment table or operating table, and the cross painted on each of the tools for stripping bark can indicate either sacrifice or resurrection). This takes place under the law of the double,[42] of binarity, or, to put it another way, of a polarity that embodies in a virtual sense both faces of an absolute opposition. Initially there is a metonymic displacement, which takes place on a bed of grease, one of the ingredients (along with felt) that the Tartars used to treat Beuys himself after his plane was shot down and thanks to which he was brought back to life, or "warmed up." This "material" not only refers to an event in Beuys's life-work but is also the sign of a kind of medical efficacy. Not only is the ability to "produce heat at will an essential element of the prestige of the primitive medicine man,"[43] but heat, to believe Novalis, is one of the keys to all therapy: "Heat and cold: these are the principles of pharmacy."[44]

For Beuys, the purpose of the piece is to reveal "our present situation" in order to raise consciousness and thereby promote progress,[45] but given the dialectic that is intrinsic to suffering and its signs and motifs, it also suggests that progress may take the form of healing. This healing consists in *doubling* the wound in order to place oneself in a situation where it is possible to resolve the injury. The remedy lies in the *repetition* of the injury, which is the only way of transcending or resolving it, because it depends on experiencing the pain, on comprehending the injury, or even just *exposing* it as a way or raising consciousness about it. Fundamentally, therefore, opening suffering up to healing depends on a certain kind of *re-presentation* of the wound, which for Beuys is essential if it is to become a cure, to be transformed into therapy. Lowenfeld argues that traumatic experiences are among the prerequisites of artistic creativity because they give rise to a constant need to repeat actively what was at first experienced passively.[46] *Show Your Wound* exhibits this "active representation," this repetition of the trauma (here collective as well as individual), in the very composition of the work, in its medical aspect: the presence of the remedy in the affliction takes the form of a doubling of that affliction. But this pharmaceutical law can also be seen at work in a medical process that Beuys invokes quite explicitly: the principle of homeopathic medicine. This of course has to do with the "therapeutic interest–one might almost say a medical-chemical-therapeutic interest"[47]–that the artist hopes to extend to the entire body politic so as not to remain a prisoner of art's "retinal destiny,"[48] since "the social organism exists as a living being in a state of very grave illness."[49] The goal is thus to treat by broadening the concept and practice of creation, by working at "social sculpture."[50] It was in this setting that Beuys began to look at homeopathy as the "therapeutic technique of the future" and brought its laws to bear directly on his works.[51]

Between 1956 and 1964 he produced a piece, today entitled *Auschwitz Demonstration*, consisting of a set of windows, one of which contains a formula that sums up the homeopathic principle: *Similia similibus curantur*. The artist offers this commentary: "It is too simple just to say 'affliction heals affliction,' even though this is true. One should rather say that illness is treated by the *signature* of illness. A poisoning can be treated by the poison that caused it. This idea originated with Samuel Hahnemann, who developed homeopathic medicine."[52] This invocation of the homeopathic principle in connection with a work representing Auschwitz, the trauma of traumas, corroborates a number of points already made, in particular the idea that emulating the suffering makes it possible not to repeat the affliction. Thus, "suffering helps man, precisely," and "anyone who strives to attend to [suffering] is constantly aware of how it can serve as a source of renewal."[53] But this can happen only on condition that the emulation of exhibited trauma is a re-presentation rather than a repetition: an "active representation" that displaces the initial form of the suffering and gives it a therapeutic orientation. Similarly, the work *Auschwitz* is supposed to contribute homeopathically to the healing of the traumatic historical event of the same name. The artist's use of the word "signature," which he emphasizes, allows us to understand more precisely the nature and process of the emulation he has in mind. Given the relation between his works and statements on the one hand

and the world and principles of alchemy on the other, Beuys is obviously referring here to the theory of the signature as formulated in the sixteenth century by Paracelsus.[54] Paracelsus based his system on the dichotomy between the macrocosm and the microcosm, in which philosophy, medicine, and alchemy combine to yield an interpretation of nature, which is "everywhere double."[55] In this vision of the world, everything is signed, everything is marked by a sign that is "like [nature's] stamp on her work."[56] This mark establishes the correspondence between the inside and the outside of each being, and in order to become a philosopher, alchemist, or physician one must learn to read these signs. These signs, "indicative of the power of transmutation, ... surround everything with a fundamental ambiguity, because everything is not only itself but at the same time something else."[57] In order to identify any given thing, one has to detect the almost infinite variety of relations, affinities, and correspondences that exist among *signata*. Reading these signs is a "living dialectic," requiring "exploration in every direction of the myriad resemblances in a world that is constantly exhibiting itself."[58] Within this world, signatures are forms[59] that, when read, become signs, which explains, for example, why the therapist must also "be supremely expert in the art of physiognomy"[60] in order to arrive at his prescriptions: the physician "identifies the remedy through its forms and figures."[61] By following the laws of this physiognomy of the world and reading signatures and their formal correspondences, the physician constructs his efficacy. Thus there should be an analogy or affinity between the affliction and the remedy (for instance, between the genitals of a sick woman and the food that can cure her)[62] because "every remedy must have the figure of the illness for which it is administered."[63] That is why the heart of a walnut, which looks just like the brain, heals words inside the head.[64]

This idea of medicine assumes that medication *emulates* the internal and external forms of the affliction by way of correspondences, similarities, and analogies among signatures. In this it respects the ancient law of healing through similarity,[65] which led the heirs of Paracelsus to embrace the homeopathic principle.[66] In any case, the important thing is to try to understand how, for Beuys, sickness can be treated by a *signature* of sickness; how this emulation of the affliction in the cure, this correspondence between the signature of the suffering and the signature of the allegedly appropriate cure, is strictly *formal*, based as it is on connections among *figures*, or, rather, on a particular register of *re-presentations of forms*, which retain something of what they are intended to work on (as the walnut repeats something of the brain) while maintaining the distinctness in principle of each sign, the irreducible difference of identity (correspondence and similarity are not the same as duplication). As Michel Foucault explains: the sign "signifies insofar as it resembles that which it indicates (or, in other words, is similar to it). But it is not the homology that it signals, for its distinct existence as signature presumably disappears in the face of which it is the sign. It is a *different* resemblance, a similarity that is close but of a different type that serves to recognize the first kind of similarity but is revealed in turn by a third."[67] What you have, then, is a vast system of affinities or of formal recapitulations marked by "a slight displacement of resemblances."[68]

By invoking the laws of alchemy and homeopathy to show how sculpture, or rather representation, can serve as medicine, Beuys thus seeks to ascribe a medical function not only to the oscillation at work in the themes, signs, and symbols that appear in his pieces and to the floating character of the various aspects of his art but also to the re-presentation that governs his plastic universe. Hence the emulation of affliction is shaped by a slight (therapeutic) displacement that prevents the initial trauma from being purely and simply repeated as work. In this way, Beuys attempts to treat the figure of the double and the dialectic around which social sculpture is structured in a wholly pharmaceutical fashion. Indeed, with the theory of signatures he is still trying to remain within the realm of forms while lending them a clinical resonance (in this respect he is absolutely, first and foremost, a plastic artist). The medical efficacy of such a formal system remains to be evaluated, however, or, to put it more precisely, the relevance of the relationship between plastic art and medicine with respect to sculpture in particular—but this requires another diagnosis from that attempted here. I shall limit myself for now to commenting on two examples of therapy, which show clearly what pharmacopoeia the artist sees himself as emulating. The first example involves the German language. Beuys, who says that "he made his way by means of language [and] did not start with so-called artistic talent,"[69] is also perfectly well aware that the orders for the Shoah—the trauma of traumas—were given in German and that its organizational, administrative, and operational structure was worked out in German. Yet he believes that the German language offers the German people a chance for "resurrection," the kind of resurrection that "follows a state of destruction affecting us all." He believes that this language will make it "possible to achieve physical healing" or what he calls "our own reanimation through language."[70] Furthermore, he offers a prescription or formula for treating the malady: "In shaping this language, we may discover that its conscious use engenders concepts and that the world, . . . as sick as it is, might well be operated on with essential concepts in such a way as to make healing possible."[71] Once again the homeopathic principle, the law of the remedy in the affliction, is called upon to represent an attempt at healing, a collective cure, sketching out a broadened concept of medicine for treating the German people with instruments that played a part in its historic trauma.

The second example involves a piece of which there are two copies, one of which is today in Dr. Speck's collection. This is a knife whose blade had its tip wrapped in a bandage. On one interpretation, this object simply illustrates a statement made by Beuys: "If you cut yourself with a knife, it is the knife that needs to be treated."[72] From a medical standpoint, however, this sick knife, which would normally—and more logically—be considered the cause of the suffering rather than the victim, serves as a commentary on and visual inversion of the homeopathic principle that governs social sculpture: if, according to the law that the remedy is to be found in the affliction, what heals the wound is also what inflicts it, then in this case that which wounds must be healed in order to go on wounding. An ironic counterpoint to Beuys's therapeutic universe, this work is therefore also, quite literally, a sick expression of it, suffering from its inability to incarnate the oscillation at work within the remedy (and the afflictions), which is supposed to deliver the wound from infernal repetition pure and simple.

## NOTES

1 Quoted in Jean Pouillon, "Malade et médecin: le même et/ou l'autre? (Remarques ethnologiques)," *Nouvelle Revue de psychanalyse*, no. 1, Incidences de la psychanalyse, Spring 1970, p. 86.
2 Clara Bodemann-Ritta, *Joseph Beuys, Jeder Mensch ein Künstler. Gespräche auf der Documenta* 5, 1972 (University of Vienna, Frankfurt am Main, Berlin, 1975), p. 96. Quoted in Axel Hinrich Murken, *Joseph Beuys und die Medizin.*
3 Erwin Panofsky, *La Vie et l'art d'Albrecht Dürer* (Paris: Hazan, 1987), p. 264. English edition as *The Life and Art of Albrect Dürer* (Princeton: Princeton University Press, 1955). See also Joseph Leo Koerner, *The Moment of Self-Portraiture in German Renaissance Art* (Chicago: University of Chicago Press, 1993), pp. 176-177.
4 "Sculpture was more than an art for traditional Chinese doctors: it was a valuable aid in physical examinations. Small, delicately carved statues, often made of jade or ivory, allowed patients to indicate the source of their pain without having to undress." *Medical and Scientific Digest*, no. 17, p. 16.
5 See the first part of Joseph Koerner's detailed and exciting analysis of this self-portrait, especially pp. 63-79 concerning the similarity between the image of Dürer and that of Christ. I take from Koerner any number of examples illustrating the persistence of this analogy in Dürer's work.
6 Koerner, *The Moment of Self-Portraiture in German Renaissance Art,* p. 179.
7 Pain is also exhibited in other works of Dürer's, including the 1511 engraving that served as a frontispiece to the *Grand Passion: Man in Pain Afflicted by a Soldier.* Indeed, according to Panofsky, "the engraving makes us 'see' the suffering that our perversity is still inflicting on Christ" (*La vie et l'art d'Albrecht Dürer*, pp. 215-216).
8 This theme was studied by Jean-Philippe Antoine in "Joseph Beuys: montrer ses blessures ou penser ses limites," *Les Cahiers de la Villa Gilet. Maladie et images de la maladie 1790-1990* (Circe, 1995). The author shows in particular how the wound manifests itself "as a singular motif unifying a repertoire of representations" and how it becomes "the fundamental motor of the representational drive" (p. 37). In general, Antoine reads Beuys in terms of a symptomatic model, with a particular focus on memory in his use of counterimages. See also his article "Je ne travaille pas avec des symboles. Expérience et construction du souvenir dans l'oeuvre de Joseph Beuys," *Les Cahiers du musée national d'Art moderne*, no. 58 (Winter 1996), pp. 51-73. My approach overlaps Antoine's to some extent in its treatment of the shaman and initiation rites.
9 *Joseph Beuys*, exhibition catalogue (Paris: Centre Georges Pompidou, 1994), p. 244.
10 A parallel between Dürer's conception of art and that of Beuys can be found in Peter Klaus Schuster, "L'Homme est son propre créateur. Dürer et Beuys ou le credo de la créativité," *Pour la mort de Joseph Beuys* (Bonn, 1986), pp. 20-25.
11 Joseph Beuys, *Par la présente je n'appartiens plus à l'art* (Paris: L'Arche, 1988), p. 19.
12 See, for example, ibid., pp. 30-43; Joseph Beuys (with Volker Harlan), *Qu'est-ce que l'art?* (Paris: L'Arche, 1992), pp. 53-55; and Joseph Beuys, *Qu'est-ce que l'argent?* (Paris: L'Arche, 1994).
13 Beuys, *Qu'est-ce que l'art*, p. 96.
14 Beuys, Kounellis, Kiefer, Cucchi, *Bâtissons une cathédrale* (Paris: L'Arche, 1988), p. 147. On Beuys's relation to Christianity, see "Entretien avec Joseph Beuys par Friedhelm Mennekes," in Max Reithmann, *Joseph Beuys: la mort me tient en éveil* (Toulouse: ARPAP, 1994), pp. 49-88.
15 Reithmann, *Joseph Beuys,* p. 63.
16 Mircea Eliade, *Le Chamanisme et les techniques archaïques de l'extase* (Paris: Payot, 1983), p. 44. English translation as *Shamanism: Archaic Techniques of Ecstasy*, trans. Willard R. Trask (New York: Pantheon, 1964). On medicine men, see A. P. Elkin, *Les Chamans aborigènes. Initiation et sorcellerie dans la plus ancienne tradition du monde* (Monaco: Editions du Rocher, 1998).
17 Mircea Eliade, *Histoire des croyances et des idées religieuses. De Mahomet à l'âge des réformes*, vol. 3 (Paris: Payot, 1983), pp. 21-22. English translation as *A History of Religious Ideas*, trans. Willard R. Trask (Chicago: University of Chicago Press, 1978-1985).
18 Eliade, *Le Chamanisme et les techniques archaïques de l'extase*, p. 39.
19 Ibid., p. 43.
20 See "Entretien avec Joseph Beuys," in Irmeline Lebeer, *L'Art? C'est une meilleure idée! Entretiens 1972-1984* (Nîmes: Chambon, 1997), pp. 87, 145.
21 Eliade, *Histoire des croyances et des idées religieuses*, p. 28.
22 Eliade, *Le Chamanisme*, p. 46.

23 "Interview with Beuys about the key events in his life by Georg Jappe," in Reithmann, *Joseph Beuys*, p. 34. On the episode with the Tartars, see also pp. 31 33.
24 Eliade, *Histoire des croyances*, p. 28.
25 Roberte Hamayon, in *Nouvelle Revue de psychanalyse*, no. 1, p. 55.
26 Beuys, Kounellis, Kiefer, Cucchi, *Bâtissons une cathédrale*, p. 160.
27 Johann J. Winckelmann, *Réflexions sur l'imitation des oeuvres grecques en peinture et en sculpture* (Nîmes: Chambon, 1991), p. 16. English edition as *Reflections in the Imitation of Greek Works in Painting and Sculpture* (LaSalle, Ill.: Open Court, 1987).
28 Ibid., p. 20. See also pp. 24-25 for a comparison of Greek bodies and modern deformities.
29 On the relation between Beuys's work and medicine, see Murken, *Joesph Beuys und die Medizin*, which contains a compendium of all of the artist's references to medicine.
30 *Joseph Beuys*, Centre Georges Pomidou, p. 243.
31 Friedrich Nietzsche, *The Will to Power*, sec. 533.
32 The quoted passage is from Claude Bernard. For an analysis, see Georges Canguilhem, *Le Normal et le pathologique* (Paris: Presses Universitaires de France, 1996), pp. 36-37. See also pp. 59 and 72 on the heuristic value of illness.
33 Friedrich Nietzsche, "Ecce Homo," *Oeuvres philosophiques complètes*, vol. 8 (Paris: Gallimard, 1974), pp. 261-263. English edition as *Ecce Homo: How One Becomes What One Is*, trans. R.J. Hollingdale (Harmondsworth: Penguin, 1979).
34 Gilles Deleuze, *Nietzsche* (Paris: Presses Universitaires de France, 1988), p. 9.
35 Friedrich Nietzsche, *Le Livre du philosophe* (Paris: Flammarion, 1991), p. 113.
36 Lebeer, *L'Art? C'est une meilleure idée!*, p. 71.
37 That is why Beuys says, for example, that "the intellectual must be shown that as a man he stands in an extremist position and that he is sick through and through. In this respect, action has a truly therapeutic character." *Par la présente, je n'appartiens plus à l'art*, p. 71.
38 Novalis, *L'Encyclopédie* (Paris: Minuit, 1966), 1074 (IV-779).
39 Ibid., 1036 (V-409).
40 Ibid., 1112 (V-333).
41 This theme has been studied by Jean Starobinski in a book called *Blessings in Disguise*, trans. Arthur Goldhammer (Cambridge, Mass.: Harvard University Press, 1993). In Starobinski's analysis of the life and work of Rousseau, many points are close to biographical details about Beuys, in particular the theme of birth as in an inaugural wound (pp. 165-166) and of "the remedy in the affliction" (p. 171). In another text Starobinski showed that Rousseau, who turned illness into a form of behavior, considered himself a "suffering healer" and that this stance made him feel close to Christ, Dionysus, and the shaman. See Jean Starobinski, *Jean-Jacques Rousseau: Transparency and Obstruction*, trans. Arthur Goldhammer (Chicago: University of Chicago Press, 1988).
42 The double motif is fundamental in Beuys's work. It has been studied by Florence Malet, "Le Corps dans l'oeuvre de Joseph Beuys," dissertation, University of Paris I-Sorbonne, 1991.
43 Eliade, *Le Chamanisme*, p. 104.
44 Novalis, *L'Encyclopédie*, 1077 (II-274).
45 Lebeer, *L'Art? C'est une meilleure idée!*, pp. 86-87.
46 Ernst Kris, *Psychanalyse de l'art* (Paris: Presses Universitaires de France, 1978), p. 29.
47 Beuys, *Qu'est-ce que l'art?*, p. 32.
48 Ibid, p. 30.
49 Ibid., p. 43.
50 "So when I say that the social organism looks bad, like a bad sculpture, the concept of art must also be capable of correcting this bad sculpture." Beuys, Kounellis, Kiefer, Cucchi, *Bâtissons une cathédrale*, p. 189. See also Beuys, *Par la présente, je n'appartiens plus à l'art*, p. 152.
51 Mruken, *Joseph Beuys und die Medizin*, p. 152.
52 "Last Space," conversation between Gaya Goldeymer, Max Reithmann, and Joseph Beuys in *Art Press*, no. 58 (April 1982).
53 Reithmann, *La Mort me tient en éveil*, p. 74. Beuys's statement, which has to do with the significance he attaches to the figure of Christ, can also be applied to the problem of suffering in general.
54 On the relation between Beuys's work and alchemy, see Murken, *Joseph Beuys und die Medizin*, pp. 133-135. Murken sees a kinship between the artist's sculpture and the theory of signatures in Paracelsus but without mentioning any text or work by Beuys.
55 Lucien Braun, *Paracelse, nature et philosophie* (Strasbourg: Association des Publications des Universités de Strasbourg, 1981), p. 104.
56 Ibid., p. 87.
57 Ibid.
58 Ibid., p. 88.
59 Paracelsus translated by Lucien Braun, ibid., pp. 120-121. On signatures, see pp. 119-127, which are a translation of fragments of Paracelsus on this question.

60 Ibid., pp. 119, 123.
61 Ibid., p. 124.
62 Paracelsus, in ibid., p. 132.
63 Ibid., p. 133.
64 Michel Foucault, *Les mots et les choses* (Paris: Gallimard, 1966), p. 42. Foucault devotes a chapter to the theory of signatures (pp. 40-45). English translation as *The Order of Things: An Archaeology of the Human Sciences* (New York: Pantheon, 1971).
65 Allen G. Debus, *The Chemical Philosophy: Paracelsus, Science, and Medicine in the Sixteenth and Seventeenth Centuries*, vol. 1 (New York: Science History Publications, 1977), p. 60.
66 Ibid., p. 117.
67 Michel Foucault, *Les mots et les choses*, p. 44.
68 Ibid., p. 45.
69 Beuys, *Par la présente, je n'appartiens plus à l'art*, p. 20.
70 Ibid., p. 19. For a critical approach to the role of language in Beuys's work, see Eric Michaud, "La fin de l'art selon Beuys," *Artstudio*, no. 4 (Spring 1997), pp. 94-103.
71 Beuys, *Par la présente, je n'appartiens plus à l'art*, p. 20.
72 Beuys, quoted in Fabrice Hergott, "L'Art comme un couteau aiguisé," in *Joseph Beuys*, Centre Georges Pompidou, p. 73.

## THE THERAPEUTIC RELATIONSHIP: LYGIA CLARK

by Thierry Davila

The difficulty of a strong option always comes down to dealing with the contradictions and ambiguities and having to pick each problem apart one step at a time.

Hélio Oiticica, *Brazil Diarrhea*, 1973

Starting in 1960, the Brazilian artist Lygia Clark produced a series of sculptures, the *Bichos* (Animals), whose aluminum parts are linked together by hinges in such a way that they can be manipulated, or *fashioned*, by anyone who picks them up, allowing their appearance to be altered at will, or at any rate within the limits imposed by the formal constraints inherent in the works themselves. The *Bichos* are undefined yet animate creatures, beings that become mobile or move owing to the intervention of the spectator-manipulator, whose role is to bring them into being, to participate in their birth. Clark characterizes each of these pieces as an "organic entity," a "living organism." She compares them to mollusks and shellfish and describes them as "essentially active works."[1] In fact, a *Bicho* is not so much a form—although each piece has genuine plastic beauty—as a set of formal potentialities, a collection of possible forms that transform the sculpture into a labile object, whose contours remain in suspense and whose identity is always open to question. It is an *open* entity, in the sense that it has no need of an "inside."[2] This is precisely what Umberto Eco means by an open work, whose configuration depends entirely on the relation that is established between what comes from outside the object (an operator) and its own inner material resources (hinges, aluminum).[3] Hence it is a creation that takes on its deep raison d'être, that truly discovers the full and virtually inexhaustible range of its forms, only by virtue of the actions of the person who attempts to explore those resources: in other words, through a *relationship* between spectator and maker.[4] The act that gives birth to the work stems from that relationship. Through other pieces created during the same period, the author was to expand the idea of this relationship in a more systematic way.

In 1963, Clark carried her exploration of openness and externalization in sculpture still further by creating a *Bicho* called *O dentro é o fora* (The Inside Is the Outside), which she regards as the culmination of her research in this regard,[5] an extreme and ultimate step. (Each phase of her work is strongly linked to the preceding phase. The *Bicho* was in a sense a spatialization of the *Casulo* [Cocoon], a folded metal work that was attached to the wall for display but projected from the picture plane in a sort of unfolding of the *Counter-Reliefs* in wood of the late fifties.) This object, also made of metal but without hinges, was "a living being open to transformations of every kind,"[6] accentuating the temporal dimension through which this series of works came into being. For by abolishing the difference between inside and outside and thus hiding nothing of what went into it (pieces of stainless steel cut, bent, and curved in various ways), this piece eliminated all that remained of a dark side or hidden face in the earliest *Bichos*. Indeed, the manipulator could invest the early *Bichos* with a brief and fleeting opacity, an illusionistic thickness or depth, merely by arranging the hinged pieces of aluminum, thereby creating a life within the object itself. *O dentro é o fora* destroys all of sculpture's interiority, and since it now has nothing to hide, it is but the instant of its transparent apparition or manipulation, "always already" open to the organicity of form; it exalts *the temporal dimension as the space of the work*. It takes on an identity that strives to be pure availability, available time—time for making, time for manipulating—for here, even more than in the early *Bichos*, as Lygia Clark says, "space belongs to time continually transformed by action."[7] (After *O dentro é o fora*, the artist created another *Bicho* without hinges, *O antes é o depois* [The Before Is the After], the title of which aptly reflects the priority she grants to the present moment in the display of her sculpture.)

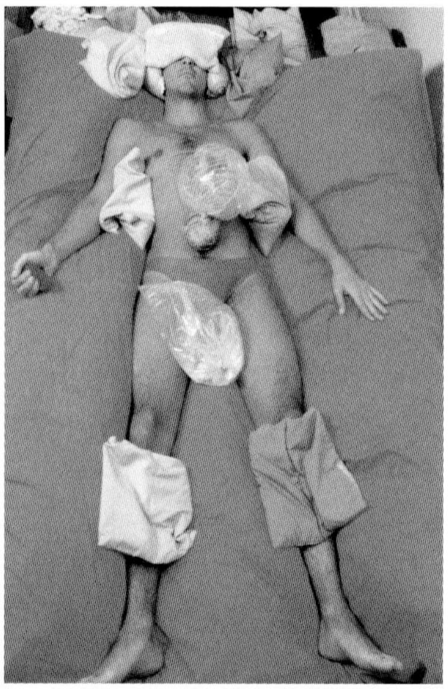

Lygia Clark, *Objetos relacionais*, 1980

The temporal dimension, as well as the relationship with the spectator—the exploration of the openness and externalization of the work—takes on another and still more precarious aspect in *Caminhando* (Moving Along), an aspect that is at once more available and more decisive. The artist tells us how to proceed: "Make the *Caminhando* yourself. Take a ribbon and cut it, twist it, and glue it to make a Möbius strip. Then take the scissors, stick the point into the surface, and cut along the length of the strip. Be careful not to cut into the existing cut, which would separate the ribbon into two pieces. When you've gone all the way around, decide whether to cut to the right or the left of the existing cut. This choice is crucial. The whole meaning of the experiment lies in the act of making it. The work is your act. As you cut the ribbon, it narrows and splits into entwined loops. In the end, the path is so narrow that you can't continue. That is the end of the line."[8] With *Caminhando*, the work exists only at the instant it is being made; it is nothing but time—the time of action—and relationship—the relationship between the paper medium and the person manipulating it. What remains of the operation, a divided ribbon, is not a relic, for a relic always implies a fetishization of the object. Nor does it represent the plastic result, since the piece exists only if someone makes it—conducts the experiment—and the "sculpture" appears only at the moment of its completion. Art is nothing but a way of pursuing an action for a certain period of time by inventing it. It is concentrated in an act that no artifact can crystallize (*Caminhando* declares the death of the object that the *Bichos* made fluid), in a living process that leaves creation in an extremely precarious position.

It is noteworthy that the questions Clark so boldly raised in the early 1960s with *Bichos* and *Caminhando* (questions of the relation between form and the spectator-author and of the exaltation of the moment) would continue to preoccupy her until the end of her life. In her last years, during which she found herself caring for deeply disturbed patients, she experimented with "borderline" therapeutic practices using "relational objects" that were also works of art. It was as if the artist's emergence as a therapist were in a sense incorporated into the very essence of her sculpture, reflecting a career that would take her from Mondrian and neo-concretism[9] to group and later individual therapy sessions intended as treatment for "specator-patients." The question was how to move from painting and sculpture to therapy based on the invented form and plastic and aesthetic practices she was developing. How and why can works of art manipulated by a creator-therapist be used to treat the physical and mental disorders of the people who experience those works?[10]

Let us return to the two elements that shaped Clark's artistic research, two elements that were the active principle of the relational objects that appeared in her work in the mid-1960s (at the very moment when she began characterizing her creations as "propositions"). She used these objects in group therapy sessions in Paris beginning in 1973 and then in an even more explicitly therapeutic setting with borderline patients from 1976 to 1984. These objects were generally made of fragile and commonplace materials, including trinkets and throwaway items such as pieces of string, bags, pebbles, stockings, tissues, sand, and so on. They had to be manipulated and applied to the body to reveal their sensory efficacy (Clark characterized them as "sensory objects").[11] Consider, for example, *Stone and Air* (a plastic bag filled with air with a stone resting on it) and *Water and Shell* (a plastic bag containing water and shells divided into two symmetrical parts by an elastic band that allowed the shells to move about inside the object). These objects did not go into action until they became part of the body that discovered them. The person manipulating them used them to reawaken his senses—to become alert—and breathe new life into ordinary commonplace gestures. Thus these pieces defied the very idea of the institutionalized museum, which is structured around a ban on touching.[12] The name given to these objects is a direct allusion to D. W. Winnicott's idea of transitional space and transitional objects (the artist was a reader and critic of Winnicott) in that they allowed for the elaboration of a neutral zone of experience through the free and indispensable intervention of the person manipulating them. The existence of the neutral zone was never challenged but rather encouraged by allowing the public access to the objects.[13] They are also related to the part objects studied by Melanie Klein. Examples of "part objects" include the breast, feces, or any other part of the body, and they are "endowed in fantasy with characters similar to those of a person (such as persecuting, comforting, benevolent, etc.)."[14] By helping the patient achieve emotional release and stimulating the return of the repressed, the artist was able to use relational objects in therapy to bring about the same type of psychic investment as that associated with part objects, despite the fact that Clark was in other contexts critical of Klein's notion of object.[15]

The psychoanalytic context in which the work evolved (which deepened the artist's understanding of what she had previously explored in "sculpture," namely, the relationship with the manipulator, the participation of the spectator-author) allowed Clark to pinpoint a fundamental problem with the identity and power of relational objects, a problem that is the essential resource of the therapeutic method she developed. This was expressed most notably in her critique of Klein's theory (as well as in her desire to "go beyond" Winnicott). Clark never stopped proclaiming the disappearance of the object,[16] its absolute and permanent death, even as she continued to use relational objects in individual and group therapy. This proclamation goes back at least to *Caminhando* (1963), but it can also be seen as related to her interest in the 1950s in the "death of the plane,"[17] which led her to spatialize geometry and free the spectator from having to face the wall, so that she might pursue by other means the organic development of art and its fusion with living movement, that is, with the movement of the body. Contradictory though it might seem, however, the elimination of the object was inextricably intertwined with its preservation in therapy in the form of tenuous, rudimentary pieces, supple, labile devices that were the source of a kind of material resistance defined by the manipulations with which they were associated, manipulations that allowed a bond to be forged between the participants. This encouraged emotional discharges that placed Clark's clinical procedure in a cathartic context. Indeed, the death of creation as artifact presupposes the presence of the relational object, which is its identity: it is a question of making the disappearance of the formal work the reason for the presence and preservation of the object and its openness to participation by the manipulator-author-patient, as well as for its effects on subjects suffering from certain types of disorder. One has to bear this contradiction, or, rather, this *problem*, in mind in order to understand how and why sculpture was able to become the "living heart" that led Clark to become a therapist.

What the death of creation as artifact does above all is to bring into play a *desubstantialization of the object*, which finds its expression in several of the characteristic features of relational objects. To begin with, relational objects are not the site of any sedimentation of meaning. They are not supposed to contain or fix or record any artistic, psychological, physical, or human truth. They can be described not as works of truth but rather as events or experiments in living and producing, which have nothing to do with the categories of truth and falsehood. Since they are in themselves nothing but pure openness, they elicit movements, processes, or actions that are alone the bearers of meaning—meaning in the process of constituting itself: an emerging life-line, which briefly takes on a plastic form as a way of experiencing itself. Meaning exists only *as act*, at a given point in time. Desubstantializing the object therefore means, first of all, not taking the work as a site of truth and its crystallization. That is why there is absolutely no fetishization of sculpture in Clark's work, and it also accounts for her indifference, and indeed her growing opposition, to the museum as institution.[18] For the museum in effect embodies the social transformation of the work into a (cultural and financial) value-bearing good, and above all the institutionalization of a distance from form (the distance of contemplation imposed by the law of value, in fact) that is incompatible with the *practice* of art as explored by the artist.

The desubstantialization of the object also involves a transformation of its psychic function related to the dramatic change in its artistic status. It is no longer the focal point of the spectator's projection, as sculpture and painting traditionally have been, but rather a means of action, a point in a trajectory, a journey, rather than a sort of Rorschach test serving as a way of reading the fundamental interiority of the subject. As Lygia Clark says: "I become aware that the *Caminhando* is my ego's initial move toward the world; I perceive rhythm as a totality, from the soccer match on the beach to Mozart."[19] Relational objects are a way of rediscovering the world as form, of belonging to that which is outside us but runs through us, while avoiding any screening phenomenon induced by matter. That is probably the reason why the vast majority of these pieces are physically diaphanous. It also explains why Clark increasingly emphasized the precariousness of her work (she invoked the "sense of the precarious" in describing *Caminhando*, and in 1983 she proposed "the precarious as a new concept of existence against any form of static crystallization in time").[20]

It is in light of this desubstantialization that we can understand the difference between relational objects and transitional or part objects. Rightly or wrongly, Clark still sees the latter as instruments of sedimentation. Transitional objects are instruments of sedimentation despite the fact that Winnicott uses them in a participatory dynamic, a relational game, because when introduced into the realm of art they nevertheless become the focal point of "a transferential poetics."[21] Part objects are also instruments of sedimentation because they suffer from a lack of openness to the subject[22] and as such continue to support the distinction between subject and object. In this critique we find once again the two basic ingredients of art according to Clark: externalization and the establishment of a relationship, an inscription of the work in the open dynamic of time, of the moment.

But relational objects, because of their promised disappearance (which is once again structurally linked to their preservation), cannot be a means of transferring meaning into the body of an artist and/or spectator-author-patient presumed to be capable of embodying it, of becoming its organic substance. On the contrary, they function only by achieving a desubstantialization of the body. That is the basis of Clark's critique of the "Body Art and Happenings" of the 1970s, from which she felt radically alienated.[23] Body art (as in the actions of Hermann Nitsch) relies on a theatricalization not found in the collective working sessions organized by the therapist-artist. Afterward, it perpetuates itself, it subsists, only thanks to the distance between the spectator and the work that relational objects are intended to destroy. Last but not least, body art fetishizes the body, transforming it into a site where the truth of art takes place. This reification of the organic led Michel Journiac, in his *Mass for a Body* (1969), to create, with his own blood, a sausage whose artistic value was supposed to be equal to that of a Christic substance (the artist's blood was to be eaten during an artistic-religious ceremony). For Clark, by contrast, the body is not so much a site of sedimentation of meaning and as such a bearer of absolute truth as it is a transitional passage to that which lies outside it. Thus, in a series of pieces entitled *Biological Architecture*, the participants act collectively, using relational objects (meshes, threads, plastic bags) to elaborate a living space and to socialize the organic. Similarly, in *I and Thou: Clothing-Body-Clothing Series*, which uses other relational objects (overalls with plastic masks allowing the manipulators, who cannot see each other, to enter into a dialog by touching, each discovering the other by tactile means), the body, according to Clark, becomes the house (these experiments in fact figured in a work entitled *The House Is the Body*). This led to a transformation not unlike an organic spatialization: "Man in this case is a living organism. He incorporates the concept of action by way of his gestural expression. He ceases to be his own object and becomes the object of the other, relating the process of introversion to that of extroversion. He inverts the concepts of house and body. Now, the body is the house. It is a communal experience. There is no regression because there is openness of man to the world."[24] Because the body sought by Clark (especially the body to be treated) is oriented entirely toward this openness to the world, it is no longer in any sense an object holding a significant content imprisoned within it. It is rather something that exposes itself to the other and allows the other to penetrate it. This desubstantialization expresses the dream of the body as pure exteriority, pure relation, the organic side of the relational object. And if there is a *Nostalgia for the Body* (to borrow the title of a set of action works from the late 1960s), this is also linked to the impossibility, or at any rate the difficulty, of mourning for interiority.

The mark of Lygia Clark's originality lay in her ability to derive therapeutic and cathartic efficacy from these desubstantializations by finding a way to bring them to light through art and in particular through sculpture. In this respect, the real formal (as well as medical, or at any rate clinical) breakthrough began with *Caminhando*, which served as the basis for group and individual therapy sessions: this work destroys the subject-object distinction and opens the way to a fusion of bodies involving the manipulator and the supporting medium.[25] The resulting participation of the "spectator" exists only because it does not confine itself to the moving hands of the author and the circles of cut paper, even if the act needs both in order to "live" at a given point in time. Creation and treatment are both forms of action involving "an object that has no value in itself"[26] but is used both to exalt the action (and the disappearance of the object) and implicate the body (and its transformation into a medium). The position of the artist-therapist grows out of romanticism: she speaks of "the romantic attitude of the artist who still feels the need of an object, even if that object is the artist himself, in order to deny it."[27] It is in any case a way of occupying the space of a *difficul-*

*ty* and making it operational so as to try to reach out to the world with an art whose intention is to heal. Here, then, we have a contradiction expressing the utopia of fusion (another name for health) and a tension that becomes a virtue, both feeding on the romanticism of direct perception without intermediate processes: "Lygia Clark devotes all of her effort... to plunging into what is contradictory, to absorbing it, to clinging passionately to that which excludes it, to trying with all her might to maintain herself in the heart of the physical world, in the entropy of the cosmos, as if she could there achieve through her work an impossible fusion with the world, from which she nevertheless knows full well we are all separated at death."[28]

## NOTES

1 *Lygia Clark* (published jointly by the Fondació Antoni Tàpies, Barcelona; MAC Contemporary Galleries of the Museums of Marseilles; Fundação de Serralves, Porto; Société des Expositions du Palais des Beaux-Arts, Brussels; Réunion des Musées Nationaux, Paris, 1997), p. 121.
2 Ibid.
3 Umberto Eco, *L'Oeuvre ouverte* (Paris: Seuil, 1962), pp. 15-40.
4 *Lygia Clark*, p. 121.
5 Ibid., p. 164.
6 Ibid.
7 Ibid.
8 Ibid., p. 151.
9 The *Manifesto of Neo-Concretism*, which a number of artists signed in 1959, declares among other things that the work of art is an organic whole. It was published in an issue of the review *Robho* devoted to the work of Lygia Clark (no. 4, 1968), and recently reprinted in *October: The Second Decade (1986-1996)* (Cambridge, Mass.: MIT Press, 1997), pp. 31-35.
10 In a letter from Rio de Janeiro to Guy Brett dated October 14, 1983, Clark discussed her success in therapy sessions. In particular, she remarked that "the more serious the case is, the more rapid the progress." *Lygia Clark*, pp. 336-338.
11 Ibid., p. 266.
12 On this point, see Didier Anzieu, *Le Moi-Peau* (Paris: Bordas, 1985), pp. 135-155.
13 "From the outset, the transitional object and transitional phenomena bring every human being something essential, namely, a neutral zone of experience that will go unchallenged." See D. W. Winnicott, *Jeu et réalité. L'espace potentiel* (Paris: Gallimard, 1975), pp. 22-23.
14 See under the heading *objet partiel* in Jean Laplanche and Jean-Baptiste Pontalis, *Vocabulaire de la psychanalyse* (Paris: Presses Universitaires de France, 1990), p. 295.
15 *Lygia Clark*, p. 322.
16 See, for example, ibid., pp. 211, 233, 264-269 "On the suppression of the object" and notes.
17 Ibid., p. 142.
18 Yve-Alain Bois tells how Lygia Clark refused an invitation for a retrospective exhibition of her work in a French museum, much to the surprise of the conservator, on the grounds that her work had nothing to do with the idea of the spectator as commonly embodied in museums. *October: The Second Decade*, pp. 27-28.
19 *Lygia Clark*, p. 265.
20 Ibid., pp. 187, 211.
21 Ibid., p. 264.
22 "In destruction, the 'relational object' is a receptacle destined to receive the subject's attacks not as an object or even a part object (Melanie Klein) but rather in an undifferentiated way: the two bodies are like connected jars, containers in which the child does not establish communication between himself and the object." Ibid., p. 322.
23 See the story told about this by Yve-Alain Bois in *October: The Second Decade*, pp. 27-28.
24 *Lygia Clark*, p. 248.
25 Ibid., pp. 151, 187.
26 Ibid., p. 152.
27 Ibid.
28 Jean Clay, "Fusion généralisée," *Robho*, no. 4 (1968), p. 12.

## ART, HEALING, AND HISTORY

by Sander L. Gilman

"Can Art Make You Give Up Smoking? Artists Create Works for The World Health Organization" shouts the press release of the World Health Organization's regional office for Europe.[1] This is an odd claim. "What do a hundred Murano glass ashtrays [by Stefano Arienti], a slice of embroidered ham [by Wilm Delvoye] and a huge blue velvet sculpture of human lungs [by Milena Dopitova] all have in common?" The World Health Organization's exhibition, held in London and other European capitals during 2000-2001, "aim[ed] to raise awareness of the health risks of smoking, the benefits of quitting, the difficulty people have in successfully quitting, and how people can be supported by health providers to quit." Can art be an instrument of health policy or can it cure? The materials for the exhibition make the goal clear. There are no claims for ethereal beauty and the sublime in this art. Rather, hard statistical reasoning: "Research has shown that 70 per cent of the UK's 12 million smokers already want to give up." And what is the role of art in helping them accomplish this? It is "to reduce tobacco-related death and disease among tobacco-dependent smokers and to prevent non-smokers from starting to smoke." If, the rationale goes, the global tobacco industry has sold us on smoking through images, then artistic images will scare and wean us from cigarettes. Postmodern art as an advertising surrogate? Twentieth-century artists such as Andy Warhol parodied the devices of advertising art. The intent here is not to highlight how advertising creates images to influence us, but to empower us with images to take control over our actions. But just to make sure, the creators of this exhibition provide us with "top tips for giving up smoking" which begin with "don't go it alone." And the person you should call on is "your family doctor, a high street chemist or another expert," but not your local art gallery or print maker or performance artist. How strange? Art cures? But "nicotine replacement therapy" is also effective, states one of the other handouts, which advocates some type of medical or psychological treatment for tobacco addiction.

Now I am not usually a skeptic when it comes to the efficacy of art. I do believe that religious art can convert the unbeliever or reinforce faith; I have experienced the thrill of weeping before a particularly moving work of art or being disgusted by it. People have told me that they have been taught moral lessons by viewing great works of art. But will a painting cure my craving for an Uppman cigar after dinner? Will Gavin Turk's video and photographs of a smoking monkey doll persuade me 1. that even monkeys can be addicted, 2. that I am no better than a monkey as I cannot reject my cigar, or 3. that I am much better than a monkey because through rational choice I can see the benefit of giving up smoking? Do these works of art really have the same power that the Philip

Morris page had for my generation (when we imagined we could be really "hip" sitting in an expensive hotel listening to him "Calling Philip Morris")? Will they grab today's Chinese, moving into the lead in world consumption of tobacco, as they follow the pied piper of the Marlboro man?

Certainly art has been seen to be therapeutic since at least the nineteenth century. (Indeed perhaps forever–David cures or at least tries to cure Saul's madness through music and Aristotle makes the same claim.) By the nineteenth century what had been folk practice or anecdotal reporting came to be systematically part of therapy.[2] Focusing one's hands and minds through various forms of work, including the making of art and poetry, was a means for nineteenth-century thinkers to image how people who were ill could be cured. This was the basis of those who reformed the mental asylums in the late eighteenth century. The therapists of the nineteenth century stressed the natural healthfulness of family and society as a means of curing the insane. Painting, writing poetry, listening to music or dancing all were undertaken within a therapy framework that took the family rather than the hospital as its model. The Quakers, especially the Tuke family in England and Philippe Pinel in France imagined that if you provided the same social context for the mentally ill as that people outside of the asylum experienced, then the mentally ill would learn to behave quite normally. If only out of shame or out of the desire to be a member of their new family as provided in the asylum. It as at least somewhat more successful than the chains and shackles of Bedlam Asylum had been. The works of art produced were seen to be indicators of a cure rather than the madness of the patient.

Today art by the mentally ill is big business. Already in the asylum of the latter nineteenth century, now run by physicians, asylum directors furthered artists whose work they saw as having aesthetic value, such as Richard Dadd, often serving as their agents. By the rise of outsider art in the 1940s under the aegis of Jean Dubuffet, the art by the mentally ill was seen as possessing a certain rare insight not open to those outside of the walls or labels of the asylum. What had begun as therapy became commodity; what had begun as a force to return the insane to the world became a rationalizing for the value of their insanity. I often reflect on how we transform our "weaknesses" into fashion, which necessarily commodifies them and imbues them with economic function. In Chicago where I now live, the best case is the outsider artist Henry Darger and his "Vivian Girls." Often institutionalized in his childhood, his art and writings seemed to have been created for the sheer act of creation, found only after his death piled in his apartment and never shown to anyone else. Art for art's sake, neither therapy nor commodity? Recently Darger has been seen as a closet pedophile or a paranoid creating an endless set of interlocking tales. When all four of the Brontes did this as a collective act, no critic saw fit to label this as anything but some type of apprenticeship for their lives as novelists. Which is the art of the insane?

Today a physician such as Janos Marton can create the "Living Museum" in the abandoned Building 75 of the Creedmore Psychiatric Hospital in Queens, New York.[3] For the past 19 years "800 men and woman have shed their identities as psychiatric patients and bloomed instead as artists." But we have moved rather far away from the idea of art as an aid to the socialization and therefore the cure of the patient. Art is not therapy for Dr. Marton. "It's art that matters." But it is a very special kind of art. People who are stigmatized, according to Dr. Marton, by the label of mental illness transform themselves when they become artists and "suddenly think of themselves as a painter or a poet." It is not "good" art, in the sense of the trained artist-patient that haunts much of the work of the 1920s, such as that of the Heidelberg psychiatrist Hans Prinzhorn, who in 1922 literally wrote the book on *The Art of the Mentally Ill.* Mental illness, following the precepts of Prinzhorn, does provide a drive to make art. It is even more the case, as Marton follows the ideology of outsider art, that the mentally ill are the true artists. He states that "you don't have to be mentally ill to be a great artist, but you definitely have to work very hard to get to a spot where mentally ill people are automatically. … The point is that art is not going to take away your mental illness. But it builds on the symptoms of mental illness. Great art really occurs in the domain where schizophrenic processes often occur." Art now is the end of the process of mental illness, rather than a cure that will restore the mentally ill to mental health.

The problem with Marton's argument, as it was with Prinzhorn's, is that much of what was produced in the asylums in the past two hundred years is neither interesting nor engaging. When he solicited works for his study, Prinzhorn asked his colleagues in the asylum that sent him works of art to send him only the best and the most interesting in the 1920s. Today Dr. Marton notes that "the idea of talent is overrated. … We are more applied modern art, conceptual art." What it does is to give the patient role meaning. And that is not too far from the idea of the reform asylum: "Suddenly the disadvantage of the patient's existence, which is time and boredom and waiting … suddenly turns into an asset." Indeed Marton's gallery-hospital "is more like a family structure, where people get what they need, not what they deserve." This is the claim of the reformed asylum but with a postmodern twist. But equally important: "People come to see your work." As in the asylum gallery in today's "Bedlam" asylum (part of Maudsley Hospital) in London, it is advertised and displayed as work by mental patients. It is precisely the stigma that attracts the audience. It is now called outsider art. It is the art of "the other," exactly that category that Marton wishes to banish from the experience of the insane.

The "other" can be positive if we romanticize it and give it status. The German expressionists did this in the 1920s having read Prinzhorn and his colleague Wilhelm Meyer-Gross, who wrote on the writings by the mentally ill. They wrote "schizophrenic" poems and made "mad" art. When Hitler came into power, he took them at their word: in the exhibition of "Degenerate Art" in 1935, he labeled all of them "mad" and "defectives" and "perverts." With their own claim he banished them from the museums, drove them out of Germany, or murdered them. They were never "mad" but they achieved status from the claim of being outsiders. Under the Nazis they quickly were treated as outsiders like those murdered in the asylum. A very different fate than being praised for being a "mad" genius. Romanticizing states of mental pain as the wellspring of genius or simulating such states within one's creative work is paradoxical. If one were very convinced that madness is the core of creativity, why would one desire to be cured?

To this point we have seen a number of interpretations across the years of the relationship between art (of all media) and illness. The claims are clear: seeing or producing art can cure illness. The ill are better artists than the healthy. Indeed illness is a form of creativity. Creativity is the result of illness. The social status of the artist is the social status of the insane. These views have been debated from the Greeks to the present. But it has a different meaning for us over the past hundred years. Western societies lost faith in the omnipresence of the divine in the Enlightenment. Today we sense that illness is a state that all have or will face and thus we try to endow it with positive meaning. For we no longer believe, as our ancestors fervently did, that only the evil or the unbeliever will be punished with madness or disease. We no longer believe that the moral will die a "good death" in the bosom of the family. When we moved the human being with all of our human frailties into the center of the universe, we began to give more and more value to illness as a common, if not universal, part of the human experience. The very special world of those who have illnesses–from mental illness to various forms of physical aliments such as tuberculosis or forms of disability–come to define all of us. For we know that no matter how moral our lives, no matter how loyal our family, no matter how true our belief, we will become ill, age, and die. The claims about art and illness have become a way of expressing the "abnormal" states for those who are (at least for the moment) "healthy" or "sane." Healthy artists paint about illness as it is one of the topics of their lives but also because of our general preoccupation with it. Individuals who are ill or disabled use their illnesses or disabilities to present an experience for all to share. And they find a ready audience.

By the beginning of the twenty-first century we have begun to institutionalize this obsession with illness as one of the true goals of art. We have given greater meaning to their relationship. Only the ill, we say, can know and express their state; only through art we can gain access to their world. Only the creative can mirror our inner preoccupation with our own decay. Art may indeed cure but only through the same means, by providing a creative conduit for the expression of an illness or disability. This was one of the claims, by the way, that caused Daniel Paul Schreber to write his autobiographical account of his madness, so well read by Sigmund Freud, at the beginning of the twentieth century. If you could write a book, so the argument went, you could not possibly be crazy. It worked for Schreber and for the young art historian Aby Warburg, who wrote his famed essay on the snake dances of the American Southwest for exactly the same purpose. The confusion about where the truth of art lies is part of our modern dilemma.

All of these beliefs are rooted in notions of either a dichotomy between health and illness, madness and sanity, or a valorization of one pole of this dichotomy or the other. You are either mad or sane and only one state can be creative. Yet we know from the work of physicians and medical sociologists that this dichotomy simply does not exist. Health and illness lie on a long scale, the calibrations of which are tiny. Today health is often not the absence of illness but a productive life with illness. Today people with chronic illness or disabilities can be "healthy." Illness can be, however, the obsessive centering of one's life on one's mental or physical state even when society or medicine terms one healthy. Franz Kafka's attitude at finally coming down with tuberculosis may be typical. He first writes about the outbreak of his illness on September 9, 1917, shortly after his first hemorrhage:

> I had a hemorrhage of the lung. Fairly severe; for 10 minutes or more it gushed out of my throat; I thought it would never stop. The next day I went to see a doctor, who on this and several subsequent occasions examined and X-rayed me; and then, at Max's insistence, I went to see a specialist. Without going into all the medical details, the outcome is that I have tuberculosis in both lungs. That I should suddenly develop some disease did not surprise me; nor did the sight of blood; for years my insomnia and headaches have invited a serious illness, and ultimately my maltreated blood had to burst forth; but that it should be of all things tuberculosis, that at the age of 34 I should be struck down overnight, with not a single predecessor anywhere in the family—this does surprise me. Well, I have to accept it; actually, my headaches seem to have been washed away with the flow of blood.[4]

Kafka was ill well before he had symptoms. Indeed, he had made illness his life's work. He too was creative, but his creativity needed his illness.

When we imagine a world in which illness exists, we must imagine a world in which all aspects of the world can be the stuff of creativity. Yet we cannot simply equate specific states of health or illness with the creative. Being ill or healthy does not provide you with insight that can be communicated to others. Only creativity provides you with the tools to capture the imagination. Illness may provide the creative person with the materials for art; it is not an automatic conduit for creativity. Indeed, the creative individual may seek out illness and so identify with it because of our claims of its importance; socially prescribed hypochondria becomes a necessity of the individual's art. Nor is the production of art as therapy the same as the production of art for inner communication. They may overlap, but they need not. Even truly bad, inexpressive, crude art can have therapeutic effects for the person producing it, just as one does not expect Shakespearean monologues on the psychoanalytic couch. Therapy is not pretty and is often very private.

Let me return to my opening paragraph. Can looking at art stop me from smoking? It might if it were part of a process of art therapy in which I "painted out" my desires. It might if works of art evoking the emotional world of the smoker addressed my own inner desires and anxieties. Can we know whether this would indeed work? No, we cannot. But the intent of art, now understood as separate from therapy, is not to alter the individual but to speak to that which is common to all viewers. In doing so it can change any one of us, but in ways now very separate from the intent or purpose of the artist. We, the viewers, own the work of art. We bring to it our desires, our needs, and our interests. We change. Rainer Maria Rilke in 1908 evoked gazing on the "Torso of an Archaic Apollo":

"Yet his torso glows: a candelabrum set
before his gaze which is pushed back and hid,

restrained and shining. Else the curving breast
could not thus blind you, nor through the soft turn
of the loins could this smile easily have passed
into the bright groin where the genitals burned."[5]

You can become the perfection of the fragmented, broken work of art we see and feel, he challenges. Imaging such an ideal leads the poet to command the reader in the final line: "You must change your life." But we at the final moment must determine how.

## NOTES

1 Press packet for the Artworks project on Smoking sponsored by the World Health Organization Regional Office for Europe, November 2000.

2 See my *Seeing the Insane: A Cultural History of Psychiatric Illustration* (New York: Wiley Interscience, 1982; reprint Lincoln: University of Nebraska Press, 1996) and *Disease and Representation: Images of Illness from Madness to AIDS* (Ithaca, NY: Cornell University Press, 1988).

3 Erica Goode, "A Conversation with Janos Marton," *The New York Times* (July 30, 2002): D1, 6.

4 Franz Kafka, *Letters to Friends, Family, and Editors*, ed. Max Brod, trans. Richard and Clara Winston (New York: Schocken, 1977), p. 543.

5 Rainer Maria Rilke, *Selected Poems*, trans. C. F. MacIntyre (Berkeley: University of California Press, 1962), p. 93.

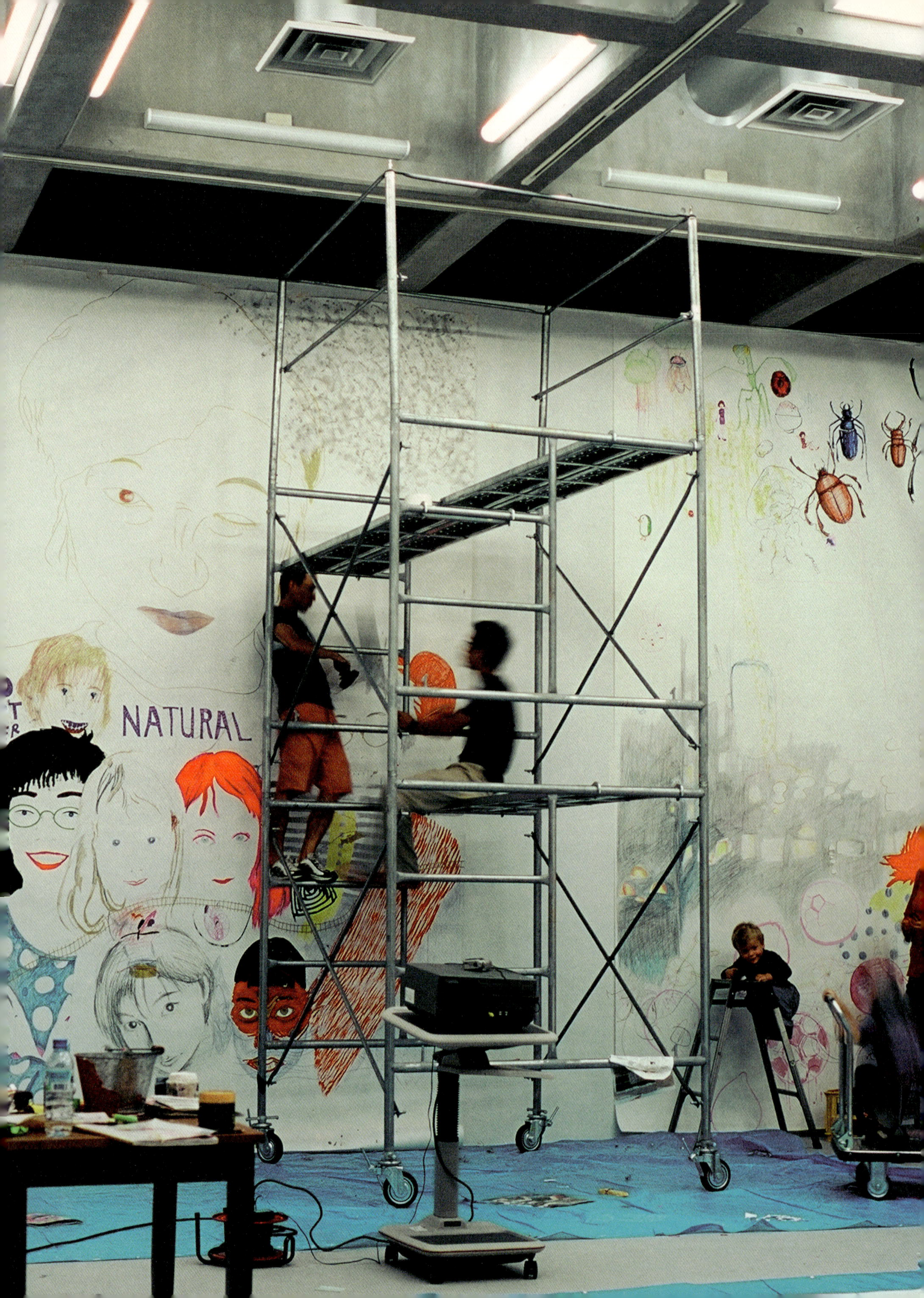
NATURAL

## ENSEMBLE

by Sandra Alvarez de Toledo

In French, *ensemble* is both an adverb and a noun. According to the *Historical Dictionary of the French Language*, "the substantivization of the adverb initially took the form of the locution *tout ensemble*" (1664), which in the realm of art referred to the unity of a work, having to do with the proper proportion of its elements. Since the eighteenth century, *ensemble* has denoted unity deriving from synchrony of movement or collaboration of various elements and was first applied to a troupe of actors (1755). By 1803, *ensemble* denoted persons or things forming a unit: *un ensemble de faits* (collection of facts) or *ensemble vocal* (vocal ensemble). In mathematics (1890), the word *ensemble* was used to translate the German *Menge* [corresponding to the English "set"—trans.], meaning a "collection of elements defined by certain unambiguous criteria of membership and possessing certain properties, and from this usage derived any number of syntagmas, such as *théorie des ensembles* (set theory), *ensemble fini* (finite set), *ensemble dénombrable* (countable set), etc., all dating from the first half of the twentieth century."

Etienne Balibar, in *La Philosophie de Marx*, made this comment on Marx's *Theses on Feuerbach*:

> The human essence is not an abstraction inherent in the singular individual. In its effective reality, it is the ensemble of social relations: *das ensemble der gesellschaftlichen Verhältnisse*. ... At bottom, the words "ensemble," "relations," and "social" all say the same thing. Whereas philosophers have traditionally adhered to one or the other of two philosophical positions, respectively called "nominalism" and "realism," here the point is to reject both simultaneously. ... For the astonishing fact is that neither of these two positions allows us to conceptualize what is essential, namely, the multiple and active *relations* that individuals establish with one another (whether of language, work, love, reproduction, domination, conflict, etc.), and the fact that these relations define what they have in common, the "genus."
>
> It is significant that Marx (who spoke French as fluently as German) here resorted to the foreign word *ensemble*, clearly in order to avoid the use of *das Ganze*, the "whole" or "totality."[1]

## INSTITUTIONAL UTOPIA

Eichgräben, thirty kilometers from Vienna. Irene and Christine Hohenbüchler live in the country, in the house in which they were born in 1964. Painted façade, sloping yard, flowers, *brute* sculpture, sheds, handiwork: a utopian rural setting, the basic given underlying their formal syntax. The studio is a little higher up, 500 meters through the woods, on the ground floor of their parents' chalet. Through the picture window the eye looks out over a dense and somber landscape reminiscent of Kurosawa. This is their territory, separated from the big

Irene and Christine Hohenbüchler, Center for Contemporary Art, Kitakyushu, Japan, 1999

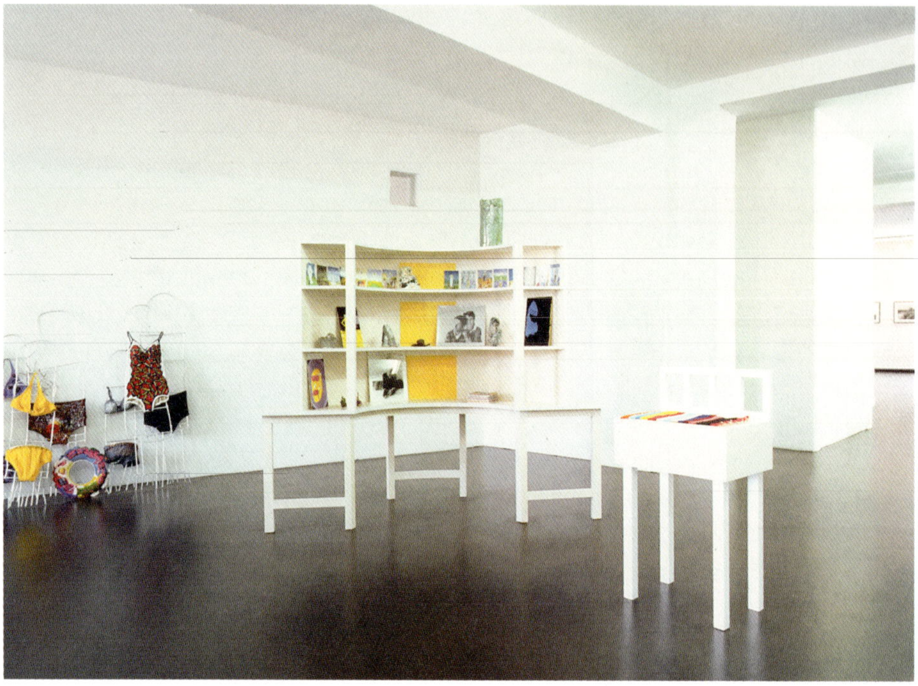

Irene and Christine Hohenbüchler, *Kommunikationsmöbel,* 1997, Documenta X, Kassel

city by the superhighway and the subway, whose stations were designed by Otto Wagner. Academy of Applied Arts, Secession, architecture, sculpture, painting: apprenticeship in history and forms. Applied Arts? Neither a vocation nor a preconception but the natural consequence of a daily tinkering (*bricolage*), four hands, more and more precise, more and more elaborate. Their current installations associate technology with "crafts," ignoring the hierarchy of art and applied arts. History, and their own family history, have made them sensitive to marginalized populations: the handicapped, the psychotic, prisoners, immigrants, victims of war. A tendency characteristic of the 1990s: art—but also advertising and fashion—"dwelt" on these margins, even though it meant diffusing and selling images, metaphors, and documents within the institutions that were most inaccessible to those populations themselves. The Hohenbüchler sisters (while continuing to show their joint work in international galleries and museums) collaborated with specialized institutions to attempt certain concrete experiments in art. One of the first of these experiments took place in Lenz, in southern Austria, with a group of handicapped adults from the Kunstwerkstatt. This joint work led to several shows, the last of which was presented in the framework of Documenta X in 1997. Between 1991 and 2003, they were invited to participate in collaborative work in Japan, Canada, Great Britain, Ireland, and Germany.

These works put them in touch with art therapy and occupational therapy. Their position on this is clear: they were not trained as art therapists and refuse to see (or instrumentalize) art as a form of treatment or reeducation. The Hohenbüchlers do not deny that a kind of analytic relationship is established to one degree or another depending on the situation and the group they are working with. But their status as artists, intervening from the outside for a limited period of time, shifts the stakes of the treatment onto the art. This displacement is at the heart of their project. Collaborative work interests them for at least three reasons: because they want to bring the collective dimension of art back into the limelight—a collective dimension that has been shunted aside since the ideological separation of art from the applied arts; because they aim (while recognizing what is utopian in their aim) to escape from *art brut*, or popular art, or "outsider art" as the Americans call it, and from the closed institutional circuit in which their rehabilitation has paradoxically trapped them; and finally, because they believe in the enigma of art's emergence. Emergence, or the childhood of art. Childhood is everywhere in their work: in person and metaphorically. The "naïveté" (etymologically, of course, *naïve* has the same origin as *native*) for which they are sometimes criticized is deliberate: it is a profound naïveté, a naïveté that welcomes otherness and strangeness in all their forms without any possibility of hierarchization or classification (hence of interpretation).

The last quarter of the twentieth century was marked by a variety of experiments in schools, hospitals, and prisons. Mostly these involved the creation of studios within these institutions, studios led either by art therapists or invited artists. In France, for example, a series of agreements between the ministries of justice and culture beginning in the late 1980s led to a policy of assigning artists

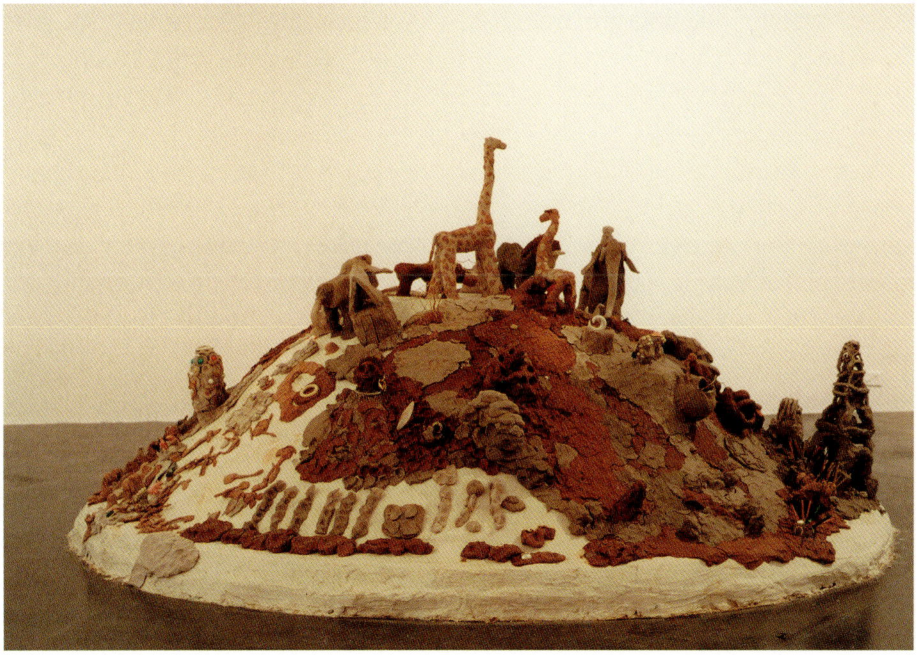

Irene and Christine Hohenbüchler, ...*pour in*..., 2000, Art Gallery of York University, Toronto

to prisons for brief studio experiments that allowed them just enough time to contrast their own individual, not to say idiosyncratic, practice with a human reality that was both outside their experience and fascinating. Running counter to this dominant current, other experiments were also attempted. In these, the common denominator was an effort to seek a different kind of relationship to the institution, that is, to the economy of space and time, to language, the body, and things: what the psychiatrist Jean Oury called an "institutional utopia."[2] In a similar vein, and in connection with the anti-psychiatry movement and institutional psychotherapy, the 1960s saw the development of new ways of dealing with mental illness in open, rural settings, rejecting all forms of medicalization and emphasizing communal spirit and "living spaces."

The workplace is decisive. Christine and Irene Hohenbüchler work as much as possible in the exhibition space, which in effect they then control. This space is precious: located at some distance from the therapeutic institution and associated with the exhibition project and the virtual presence of an outside public, it already presents itself as an *outside*. There, in the course of the daily routine, they establish their own institutional rules but do not explicitly formulate or enforce them. "The goal is to construct a space for an *encounter*," says Pierre Fédida of the therapeutic situation.[3] Here, what is organized is a living space, with schedules, movements, and spaces within spaces. Meals establish the rhythm of the day. The exhibition is constructed little by little, at a pace which respects both pathologies and the time allotted for completion of the project, which the artists insist, as a condition of their participation, must be no less than four weeks. The form that the exhibit takes is determined by the accumulation of a large number of diverse objects, materials, and tools: paintings, pearls, fabrics, wool, wood, photographs, pencils, notebooks, computers, etc. This is what Claude Lévi-Strauss calls the mythopoeic "treasure" of the *bricoleur*, or tinkerer. Assembling, tinkering, *bricolage* or *bris-collage* (breaking and gluing back together, as it were), in which Jean Oury sees the "psychotic's ability to reconstruct the world."[4]

The project is built on-site, seldom conceived in advance. In Toronto (2000), with the handicapped of the Muki Baum association, the installation took the form of huge collective drawings made directly on the wall and plaster hills 1.5 meters in diameter, which the participants covered with clay figurines sculpted on-site. The workspace became a landscape, a new territory and living space with its own topography, ludic and grotesque. The Documenta X installation of 1997, the result of work with the handicapped artists of Lenz, was designed as a living space, a combined domestic and work space. "Inhabiting" is one of the major themes in the work of the Hohenbüchlers. In material terms, this sometimes takes the form of an interior space, sometimes of an architectural form, a protective envelope for the body. For the Sonsbeek demonstration in 1993, they asked to work with the inmates of De Berg Prison. The prisoners' paintings were housed in man-sized wooden cones, whose copper cupolas mimicked the shape and material of the prison roof. The spectator, placed in the situation of a guard in the panoptical prison, had only visual access to the interior of the cell through a series of small windows. The double-hexagonal shape of the *Mutter-Kind(er)-Haus* constructed for the 1999 Biennale in Venice with the aid of Martin Feiersinger and dedicated to the victims of the war in Kosovo was inspired by their childhood cabin. This type of emergency architecture (which they associate with the work of the Japanese architect Shigeru Ban) combines their interest in organic forms with technical ingenuity and humanitarian action.

What is utopian is the impulse to create a passage between closed institutions, confined within their exclusive specialties, be they artistic or therapeutic. It is the desire to move human beings and their works from "places provided for," to borrow a phrase from the French teacher and poet Fernand Deligny, to new situations, open to exchange and to the unusual. "I have no intention of educating anyone," said Deligny of the delinquent and psychotic youths placed in his charge after World War II. "My intention is to create conditions favorable to allowing them to escape and to live."[5] In this sense, one can say that the Hohenbüchlers project has a pedagogical and therapeutic value. On the artistic plane, these attempts are the expression of a position which, because it refuses the question of *criteria*—under what conditions is this art, and who decides?—accepts neither the ghettoization of marginal artistic productions nor an elitist definition of art.

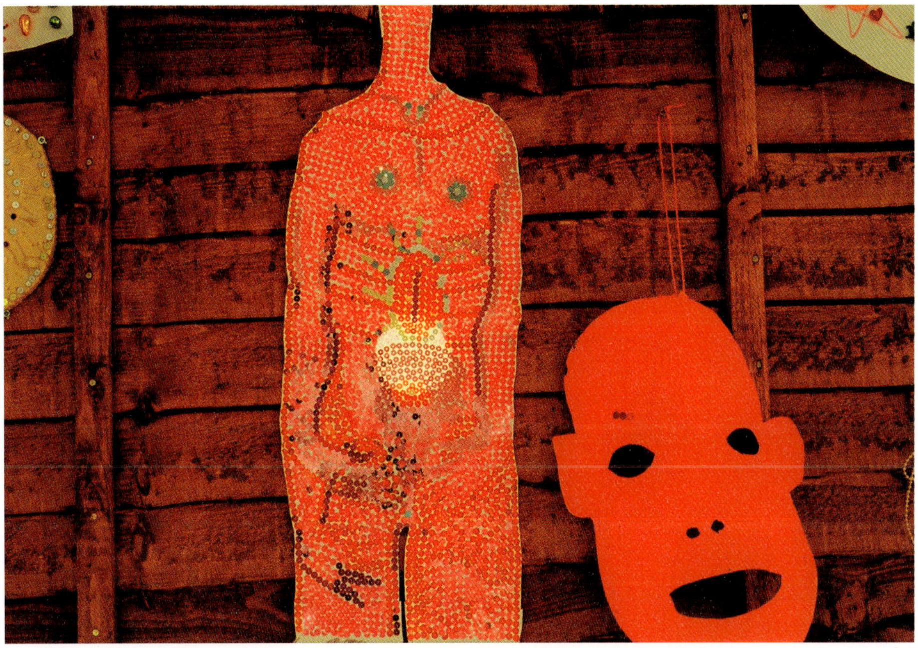

Irene and Christine Hohenbüchler, *If we all peel the onions*, 2000, Camden Art Centre, London

### AFTER L'ART BRUT

The critical fortunes of *l'art brut* were such that all production linked to mental illness and marginality is still associated with it today. It was inevitable that certain of the Hohenbüchlers' collaborative works (as well as some of their personal works, particularly those having to do with the applied arts) are also classified as belonging to what has paradoxically become a genre. Their practice in dealing with commissions from specialized institutions is nevertheless quite different. As we have seen, it is first of all a collective practice and a social practice. The idea that genius is inspired by madness and that madness carries within it the seeds of genius was prevalent in the nineteenth century, particularly in literature. The interest of art historian and psychiatrist Hans Prinzhorn in the art of schizophrenics (a term coined in 1911 by Eugen Bleuler) had nothing in common with Romanticism, however. In order to clarify what he called the "chaos of contemporary art," he set out to collect and study certain artistic products that were supposed to reveal in a pure, primordial, and authentic state the very process of creating a form (*Gestalt*). Nevertheless, the consequence of his research was to bring to light a number of unusual works and, along with them, individuals, not to say personalities: *Bildnerei der Geisteskranken*, published in 1922, devoted more than 150 pages to the lives of "ten schizophrenic creators." Walter Morgenthaler's earlier monograph on Adolf Wölfli, published in 1921, focused directly on the work that Wölfli did in the Waldau asylum from 1895 on, as well as his slavish existence as a member of the rural subproletariat in the region of Berne.[6] The *Cahiers de l'art brut*, published in the 1960s under the auspices of Jean Dubuffet, came out in the form of a series of monographs. The madman or marginal individual attained subject status through art. Adolf Wölfli, Auguste Forestier, Aloïse Corbaz, Gaston Chaissac, Henry Darger, Bill Traylor, and August Walla became the torchbearers and promoters of *l'art brut*.

The Hohenbüchlers share not only with Prinzhorn and Dubuffet but also with the Surrealists an interest in the unconscious processes at work in artistic invention and a concern with spontaneous untutored forms (though today, with the selection of certain strong works from the Heidelberg collection, one recognizes artists who have received advanced technical or artistic training, and it is always worth asking whether certain works were "encouraged" by the institution). The Dutch artist Constant recently observed that the Cobra group (contem-

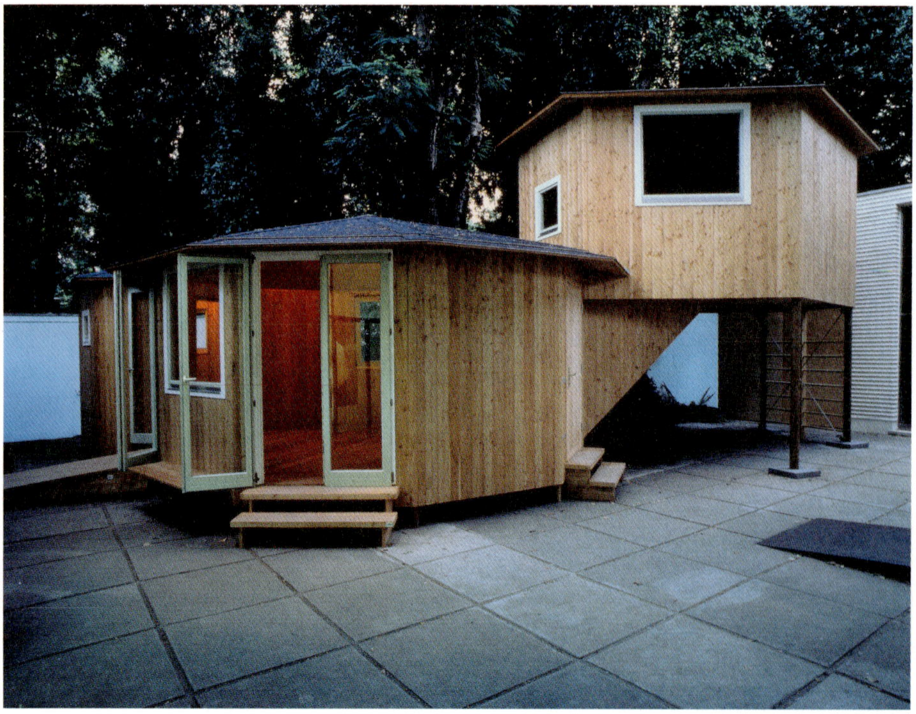

Irene and Christine Hohenbüchler, w/ Werner Feiersinger, *Mutter-Kind(er)-Haus*, 1999, Venice Biennial

porary with the creation of the Compagnie de l'Art Brut) took an interest in the "spontaneous expression of humanity," and especially in children's drawings, because of the human and artistic "emptiness" left behind by World War II.[7] It would not be surprising if the global extension of neoliberal policy and the standardization of a brand of contemporary art even less in tune with the real than it thinks it is, in colonizing images of "elsewhere," at some point reawakened the same vital reflexes. The applied arts, and the experience with "making" that their practice entails, would then eventually come in for reconsideration.

*L'art brut* was contemporary with a project of "de-alienation" of psychiatry that opened up new perspectives on madness not only in the realms of psychiatry, philosophy, and politics but also literature and art.[8] Civil society familiarized itself with the image of the madman and with the idea of his artistic potential—more, indeed, than with the madman himself. The Prinzhorn collection, before being confiscated by the Third Reich, circulated among European museums. It has recently been shown in the United States and Europe. Jean Dubuffet's collection is today housed in the Musée de l'Art Brut in Lausanne. The institutionalization of these artistic productions allows them to be seen by a broad segment of the public but runs the risk of confining the work to a separate, subsidiary space and time, which was also the fate of the mad in mental hospitals. Institutionalization created a market: works circulated and were published, shown, and sold in galleries or at auction. *L'Art brut*, as it is still called, has its stars and its rankings. The Gügging Artists House, created in the early 1980s on the grounds of an Austrian mental hospital, now has an art gallery that plays host to collectors from around the world. The works of these artists (including August Walla, who died there in 2001), most of them elderly and psychotic, are encouraged by their "managing director," the psychiatrist and artist Johann Feilacher, who ensures their "success" while at the same time alleviating their symptoms, or so he claims. The "best" drawings and paintings thus pass directly from the violently autistic imaginations of these artists to the well-upholstered spaces of *art brut* collections without touching the real, which is to say, without confronting other languages.

By showing with these artists in the institutional spaces of contemporary art, the Hohenbüchlers hope to take them out of the categories of the universal and timeless that mask the concrete fact of their isolation and specialization. They understand, however, that if this confrontation is too abrupt, it may lead to misunderstandings, thereby doing a disservice to works that critics might be tempted to classify before they have really looked at them. Yet the rhetoric of *art brut* is no more caricatural than that of institutionalized contemporary art; there is simply a tendency to stigmatize one more than the other. One way the Hohenbüchlers have found of disarming this prejudice and bringing these works into the circuit of contemporary art for the sake of their intrinsic artistic qualities is to "frame" them, that is, to inscribe them in a resolutely contemporary space expressive of the collective project. For the Camden Arts Center show of 2000, a series of display easels of wood and cork bearing objects made by the patients created a sort of script that instantly established distance around what would otherwise have been only a collection of *art brut* objects. At Kassel in 1997, the drawings, weavings, and ceramics of the handicapped artists of Lenz shared space with the project documentation in the form of videos and archives of texts and drawings. These *art brut* objects fit perfectly into an installation organized around furniture combining the rigor of the Viennese Secession with the refinement of a deliberately impoverished design. They did more than just fit in: they added a concrete and poetic dimension of otherness by creating a slight disjunction.

The Hohenbüchlers are vulnerable to misunderstandings; they are aware of this and suffer from it. The patients do not always understand their position as nontherapeutic artists. Some art therapists and medical personnel criticize them for taking advantage of the work of patients. Art professionals often do not see the profound but modestly formulated political intent of their statements, an intent that they would readily recognize in images dealing with the homeless or with postcolonialism. All this is evidence that social reality is entitled to a place in the art world only on condition that it submit to well-defined aesthetic codes, and that mental illness and to an even greater degree handicaps (which do not benefit from the "aura" of schizophrenia) are not yet included among the accepted categories of social reality.

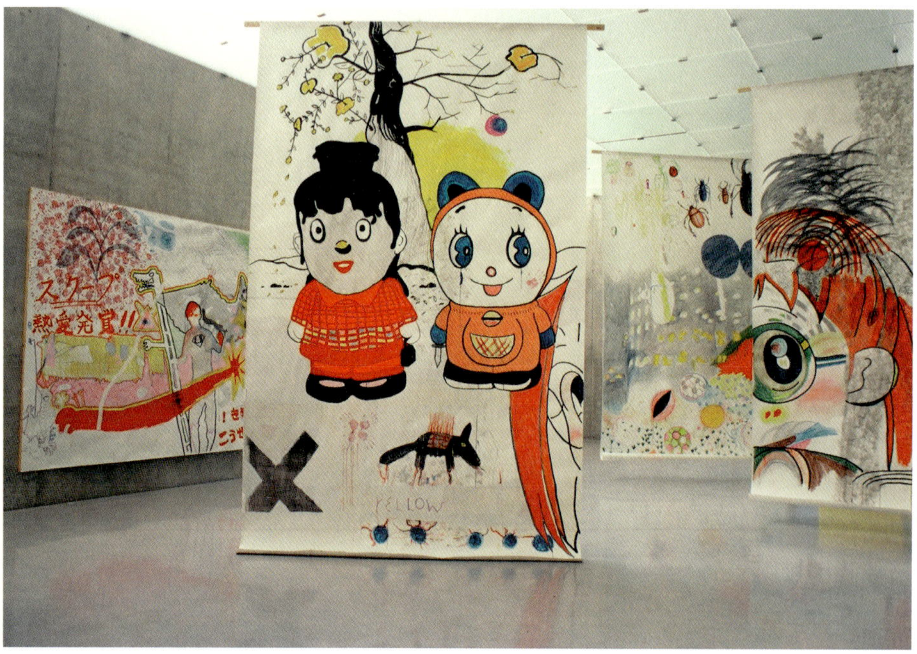


Irene and Christine Hohenbüchler, Center for Contemporary Art, Kitakyushu, Japan, 1999

**MULTIPLE AUTORENSCHAFT**

By raising the question of the onlooker who makes the work, and therefore the work of the author, Marcel Duchamp initiated a reflection on art that marked the art of the twentieth century. Yet the collaborative works of the Hohenbüchlers must be situated not so much in the line of conceptual strategies deriving from

Duchamp as in the history of the applied arts. In the title they chose for these works, *Multiple Autorenschaft*, the word that needs to be pondered is not so much *Autorenschaft* as *Multiple*, which they obviously preferred to the collectivist and therefore militant connotations of "collective." In "the multiple," the individual subject does not disappear, does not melt away. He or she coexists with others. The author multiplies himself, presents himself as a complex being, whose languages correspond to one another through a system of visual and psychic associations.

The juxtaposition of two photographs reproduced in the book *Bauhaus Textiles* by Sigrid Wortmann Weltge suggests an avenue of reflection: the first depicts the dining room of the *Haus am Horn* designed by Georg Muche; the second portrays the showroom of the weaving and pottery studio.[9] The two images are contemporary. They were taken at the 1923 Bauhaus exhibition in Weimar. The first precisely conveys the appearance of "design." The furniture of Marcel Breuer, produced and sold on an industrial scale, is associated with the aesthetics of a movement, De Stijl. The arrangement of the pieces, coupled with the architecture, brings out the image of a décor in which man's place is at once central and virtual. The second image evokes a room in an ethnographic museum, where, despite the organization of space and the resolutely modern architecture, the wall tapestries and ceramics in glass cases exclude any reference to design or décor by preserving the character of the objects as applied art, bearing a "craft" stamp. By opting for industrialization, the Bauhaus paradoxically played a decisive role in separating design from the applied arts. At the time, this separation partially coincided with the separation of male and female activities. The name Marcel Breuer is internationally known. Gunta Stölzl, Gertrud Arndt, and Monica Bella-Broner, the Bauhaus weavers, are less wellknown.

The Hohenbüchlers' installations combine and play with both orientations, design and applied arts. The Viennese Secession is a source of direct inspiration, which they do not hesitate to call upon. The Secession itself, and Joseph Hoffmann in particular, like William Morris and the Arts and Crafts Movement, rejected mass production and aimed to restore the value of traditional culture and craftsmanship. (They did not, however, share Morris's commitment to socialism as an intellectual and activist. This aspect of his work is completely neglected today, despite the 1984 exhibition at the London Institute of Contemporary Arts, which highlighted the political dimension and its contemporary relevance.)[10] References to Austrian national history, whether respectful or ironic, are not what the Hohenbüchlers are about: they shift, reinvent, and adapt those forms to a contemporary aesthetic and sensibility. Nor do they mobilize the applied arts for their own sake, to signal an outdated, anti-modern position, a "return to." The items of furniture are figures in space, somewhere between sculpture and functional objects, ludic and anthropomorphic. The high openwork backs of the chairs in the *Kommunikationsmöbel* join in a single head (a burlesque allusion to twinship) traversed by the flowing colors of a woven cover with a "Bauhaus" geometric motif. The paintings and drawings borrow their motifs and enigmatic symbolist atmosphere from Gustav Klimt and Koloman Moser (with more ingenuity and less sexuality), and some bear a dedication to the poet Sylvia Plath. Using sounds, dreams, quotations, and commonplaces, Christine and Irene Hohenbüchler have invented a language (and a typeface) whose cryptic signs they weave and trace into the fabrics and onto the pieces of furniture and the floor. Their experiments with the emergence of art among untutored or "native" artists (André Breton) strengthens them in their own psychic activity, which they aim to preserve from the cultural rhetoric of contemporary art.

The Surrealists saw madness as a subversive mode of access to the miraculous, a plus for literature and for art. The Hohenbüchlers are less scholarly and more modest in their way of apprehending both the social and psychic dimensions of the phenomena that interest them. They do not think like *auteurs* and do not seek out the individual mark of the author in art. Art is for them a common practice, an "ensemble" practice, natural, permanent, anthropological; a necessary relation to the world, to materials, to bodies, to others, and to oneself. Such is the utopia—a vision rather than a dream, according to William Morris—that is the basis of *Multiple Autorenschaft.*

## NOTES

1 Etienne Balibar, *La Philosophie de Marx* (Paris: Editions de la Découverte, 1993), pp. 28-31.
2 Jean Oury, "Utopie, atopie et eutopie," (*Chimères* no. 28, Spring-Fall 1996).
3 Pierre Fédida, "L'informe agissant, la mise en oeuvre de l'informe," in the proceedings of the colloquium connected with the show *L'art médecine*, Musée Picasso, Antibes (Réunion des Musées Nationaux, 1999-2000).
4 Jean Oury, *Il, donc* (Paris: Union Générale d'Editions. Collection 10/18, 1978), p. 120.
5 Fernand Deligny.
6 Walter Morgenthaler, *Madness and Art: The Life and Works of Adolf Wölfli*, translated with an introduction by Aaron H. Esman (Lincoln: University of Nebraska Press, 1992).
7 Benjamin Buchloh, "A Conversation with Constant," in *The Activist Drawing: Retracing Situationist Architectures from Constant's New Babylon to Beyond*, Catherine de Zegher and Mark Wigley, eds. (New York: The Drawing Center, 2001).
8 The term "de-alienation" was invented by the Communist and Surrealist psychiatrist Lucien Bonnifé, who played a key role in the transformation of classical pyschiatry starting during World War II at the Hôpital de Saint-Alban in the south of France.
9 Sigrid Wortmann Weltge, *Bauhaus Textiles: Women Artists and the Weaving Workshop* (London: Thames and Hudson, 1993), pp. 62-63.
10 *William Morris Today*, Institute of Contemporary Arts, London, 1984.

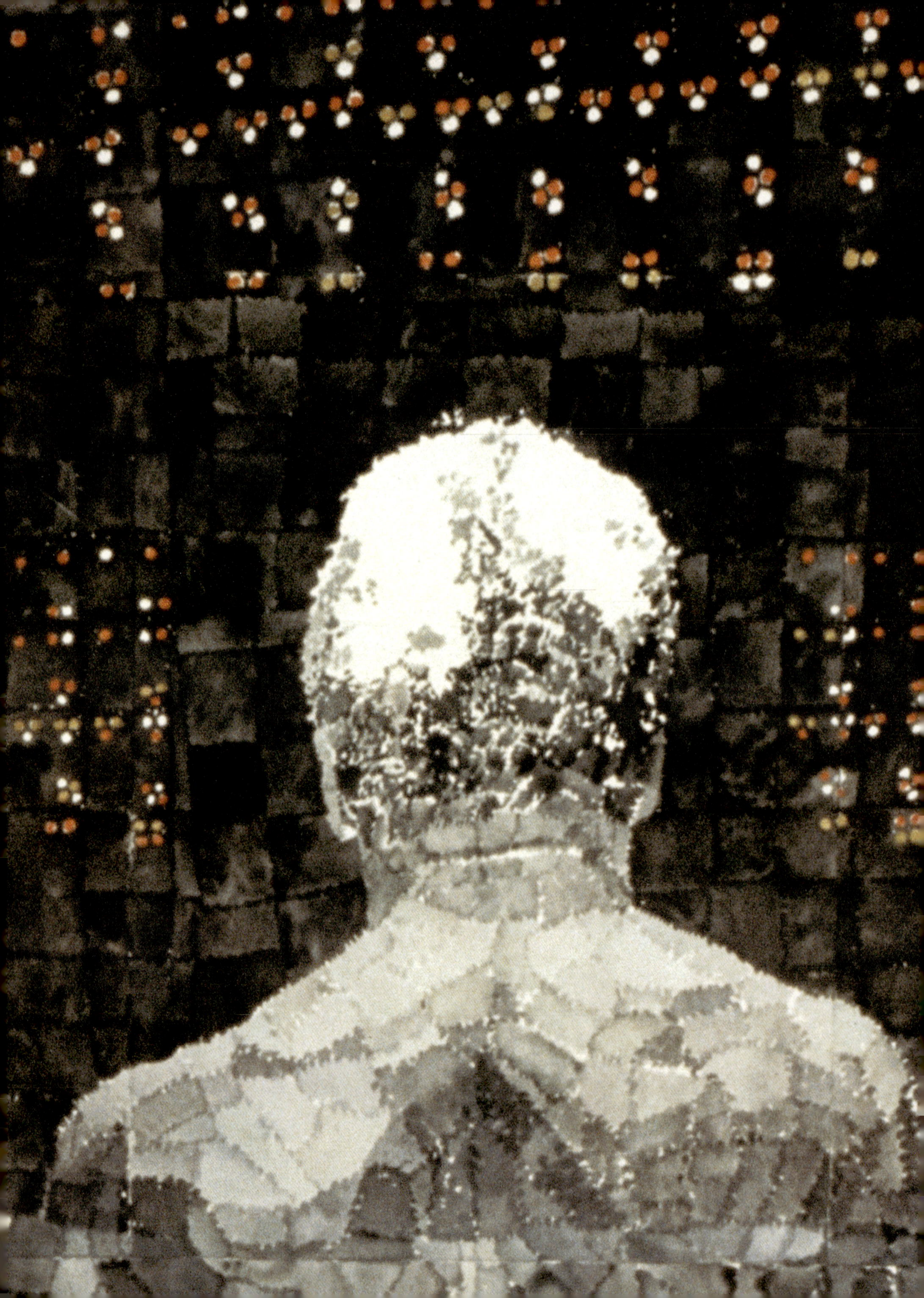

# MOJO HAND: HISTORY, HEALING, AND HOODOO IN THE WATERCOLORS OF RICHARD YARDE

by Gwendolyn DuBois Shaw

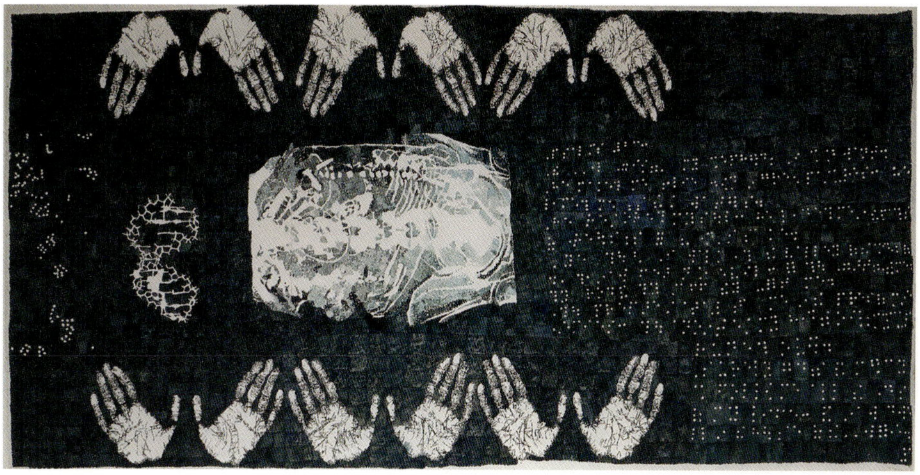

Figure 1: Richard Yarde, *Mojo Hand*, 1995-96

In 1995, as he lay ill with kidney failure, Richard Yarde began to work on a watercolor that would prove to be a dramatic shift in his artistic vision. The piece, a large, rectangular watercolor that he called *Mojo Hand* (figure 1), was born from the dreams that had come to him while lying in his sickbed at home in Northampton, Massachusetts.[1] After having tried unsuccessfully to visually represent these dreams in their specificity, he shifted to a more emblematic approach, gradually identifying and selecting important images that repeated from dream to dream, night after night. As the painting took shape five distinct elements emerged out of the white space of the paper, each one bound within a fabric of interwoven indigo blue squares. Six pairs of hands, shown palm-up; a diagram of a DNA molecule; an enigmatic grouping of dots; an X-ray of the torso of a pregnant woman; and the 23rd psalm, written in Braille. The ancestral counterpart for each element had first appeared in a dream, before being contemplated, researched, and revealed on the heavyweight, richly textured paper.

In many ways *Mojo Hand* was a breakthrough piece for Yarde. It marked a significant change in the content of his paintings, which for the preceding three decades had been records of the cultural and political history of the twentieth-century Diasporic African experience. His evocative watercolors recorded Malcolm X speaking in the Grove Hall neighborhood of Roxbury in the early 1960s, or reinterpreted an iconic photograph of the controversial turn-of-the-century boxer Jack Johnson on an epic scale. He painted culturally resonant subjects as diverse as United Negro Improvement Association leader Marcus Garvey on parade in Harlem and made a lifesize installation of dancers cavorting at the Savoy Ballroom as a part of a continuous body of work that celebrated a tangible image world that was lived and experienced, both firsthand and through popular culture.

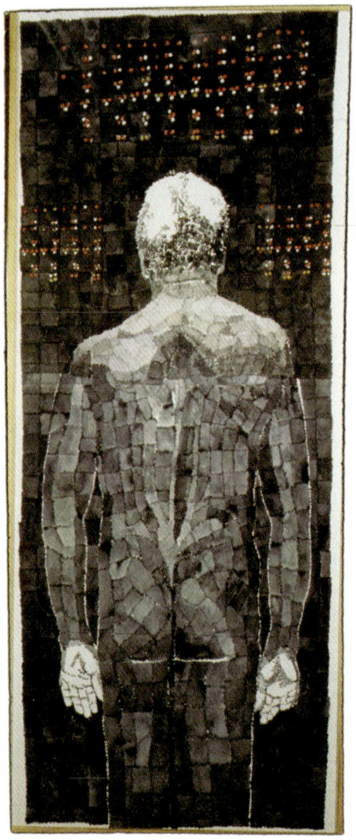

Richard Yarde, *Back*, 1993

While the mystical world revealed in *Mojo Hand* was new territory for Yarde, the medium of watercolor and the color blue were as much a part of him as his signature. Ever since childhood, when his mother enrolled him in art classes at the School of the Museum of Fine Arts, Boston, it had been his medium, in part because he enjoyed the challenges it presented, its unforgiving nature, but also because of its affordability. As with many young artists, money was a constant issue in Yarde's early career. Thankfully his prodigious talent did not go unrecognized and his undergraduate study at Boston University was facilitated in part by the support that he received from his professor, the Iowa-born artist Conger Metcalf.[2] Following graduation in 1964, Yarde enrolled in the MFA program at BU, finishing a year later. Metcalf continued to be a strong advocate for his student's work and would regularly attend Yarde's exhibition openings.[3] But if his paint choice was in part dictated by the material conditions of being a working artist in the 1960s with a young family to support, he in no way sacrificed the grandness of his vision by making little paintings. In general his works have always been large in scale, eschewing the notion that watercolor is an intimate, portable mode by which the temporal and the immediate can be recorded.

As Yarde struggled to survive the kidney failure that years of medication for hypertension had created, he began to seek hope in alternative healing communities, and as he began to work on *Mojo Hand* all this changed. While waiting for an organ transplant he found solace in the "laying on of hands" that is central to many holistic approaches to healing.[4] He investigated Central and West African beliefs about the magical worlds that control health and illnesses, taking both a visual and intellectual interest in the traditions that were disseminated across the New World through slavery. Yarde moved from venerating and inscribing the past to probing and interpreting the supernatural. By attending to the messages that his unconscious was sending him, by painting this new dream world that was born of pain and corporeal doubt, he was able to dedicate concerted attention to his own spirituality and the religious practices of the African Diaspora. Through an interrogation of the syncretic Black folk medicine and spiritual culture that still permeates the Caribbean and the Americas, the core of *Mojo Hand* emerged as a visual exploration of universal issues of mortality and transcendence.[5]

Although the popular meaning of the word "mojo" has been affected by its use in popular culture, its traditional meaning has to do with the ability of a specially made charm to do magic, to have mystical powers that will aid its owner. *Webster's Dictionary* defines *mojo* as "[prob. of African origin; akin to Gullah *moco* witchcraft, magic, Fulani *moco'o* medicine man] chiefly South, a voodoo spell or amulet."[6] In practice, *mojoes* are charm bags made out of variously colored flannel and filled with several different components depending on what they were used for, in Haitian vodou they are called *paket kongo*, or bound medicine packets, and have their roots in the Kongo magic and healing traditions of West Central African. These conjurers charms are often used to attract the affection of another as in blues lyrics such as Preston Foster's classic "I Got My Mojo Working." As performed by Muddy Waters and others, the song begins,

> I got my mojo workin' but it just don't work on you
> I got my mojo workin' but it just don't work on you
> I wanna love you so bad, child, but I don't know what to do
>
> I'm going down to Louisiana, gonna get me a mojo hand
> Going down to Louisiana, gonna get me a mojo hand.
> Gonna have all you women under my command.

However, this type of charm only touches on the broader power of mojo charms. In his seminal work, *Hoodoo—Conjuration—Witchcraft—Rootwork,* folklorist Harry Middleton Hyatt discusses the term *mojo* in the section titled "Hands, Magic Helpers" as an "object or act, which aids a person in obtaining a desire," a desire specific to them alone. Hyatt explains that "Aladdin's lamp was not a hand because anyone could rub it to activate the indwelling spirit," but a *hand* is "dressed, powered for [the owner] alone." *Mojo* joins *toby, guide, shield, roots,* and *jomo* (a transposition of *mojo*) as a term commonly used for a *hand.*[7]

The placement of the twelve hands in Yarde's painting is in dialogue with various New World and Diasporic African cultural traditions of using images of hands, both upraised and downward pointing, as protective devices. Within African American hoodoo the upraised *Helping Hand,* similar to the popular Catholic hand of power, or *Mano Poderosa,* is often found on candles and curio labels. Downward pointing hands are found in syncretic New World culture as well, for example the *milagro,* or miracle, charms frequently used in Mexico.[8] Unlike these kinds of iconic curios, the twelve handprints in *Mojo Hand* are not repetitions of a single model; instead they are individual handprints, each with their own unique lines.

While the palm prints in *Mojo Hand,* made up of the unpainted white space of the paper, are positioned in the manner of Christian benediction and hoodoo prayer, the texture of the small indigo squares mirrors with African fabric tonalities.[9] In the way that it visually recalls the rectangular format of West African strip cloth, both made by the Ewe people of Ghana and Togo and the Kente cloth made by the Asante people of Ghana, it references the spiritual source, the site from which all syncretic action issues. Each small square of paint, one rubbing up against the next, edges blurring together as they overlap, forms a visual pattern that serves as a repetitious back beat to the forms that populate its surface. And while the elements appear to float upon the underlying grid of blue paint, it is really the grid that sutures them together, just as threads of lace knit empty space into evocative designs.

From between the two rows of handprints, the other elements that comprise *Mojo Hand* emerge out of the cloth/paper left unexposed to pigment. The largest element, a found X-ray of the torso of a pregnant woman truncated to show the skeletal makeup of the shoulders and lower pelvis, glows bright white at the center. To the right of the mother's backbone can be seen the stacked vertebrae of the fetus, its ribs nestled along her hip. By placing a skeletal image between the hands, Yarde implies that this woman's body is the focus of their energy, and the skeleton in turn takes on magical import. The skeleton is the part of the body, the single system, that can withstand the ravages of time and that recalls the body's power, its existence, long after the loss of life.[10] In this way, Yarde's inclusion of the X-ray image can be seen as more than a record of a medical procedure; rather, it becomes a reference to the core of the body's temporality. This is the true interior view of life recreating itself at a structural level. And yet, in the X-ray's creation, in its existence as a record of a medical procedure not normally undergone by healthy pregnant women, lies a warning that there may be something wrong with the mother or the fetus. It is an image of the Madonna and Child and it is a premonition of the Pietà when Mary will once again hold her son after his mortal death. In this way *Mojo Hand* becomes Yarde's Diasporic African *Shroud of Turin* (figure 2). And like the mystical burial cloth that is believed to have recorded the features of the dead

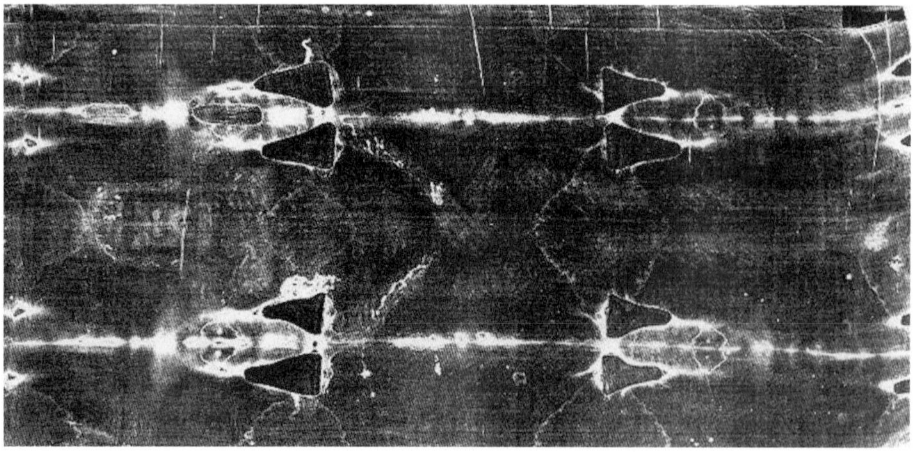

Figure 2.
*Shroud of Turin.*
Found at
http://www.shroud.com/.

Christ as his soul passed through it, *Mojo Hand* is a text of faith, pain, and transcendence.

Beside the ghostly image of the X-rayed torso, where the body's head would be, lies the small diagram of the double helix of DNA. The links between its twisting components are fragmented, broken in spots, overly built up in others. Just as the X-ray hints at danger, so too does the mangled DNA. But it also works as a dedicated code, one that describes a unique biological form; it is a blueprint for life. Here, emerging from the blue textural grid of *Mojo Hand*, the double helix (made up of 23 elements) marks the existence of life and its infinite variations. It signals the constant mutation inherent in the evolutionary process, the method by which we are all marked as individual, a point that is further emphasized by the two rows of hand prints that border the upper and lower edges of the composition.

The rendering of the 23rd psalm in Braille, to the left of the torso, continues this interrogation into the metamorphosis of the body, examining its fragility and its resiliency. By presenting Braille, a necessarily three-dimensional entity, on the planar surface of watercolor, the sense of touch is denied. This transposition underscores the need for "helping hands" to take over the job of seeing and reading what the eyes no longer can, or have never been able to do. And the *psalm*, an anagram for the *palms* that line the top and bottom of *Mojo Hand*, speaks of the safety and guidance that comes from faith.

The Lord is my Shepherd; I shall not want.
He maketh me to lie down in green pastures:
He leadeth me beside the still waters.
He restoreth my soul:
He leadeth me in the paths of righteousness for His name's sake.

Yea, though I walk through the valley of the shadow of death,
I will fear no evil: For thou art with me;
Thy rod and thy staff, they comfort me.
Thou preparest a table before me in the presence of mine enemies;
Thou anointest my head with oil; My cup runneth over.
Surely goodness and mercy shall follow me all the days of my life,
and I will dwell in the House of the Lord forever.

The familiar text of this psalm, so often recited by those suffering from illness, acutely aware of the fragility of mortality, serves as a comforting hand in its invocation of the Shepherd who leads his flock. In this way, the guiding hand of the Lord, helping those in need, that is found in the 23rd psalm is similar to the belief in the power of a "mojo hand" in New World, African American religious practices such as hoodoo.

The fabric-like dark blue watercolor background from which the ghostly forms of *Mojo Hand* emerge not only ties together the hands, bones, and braille dots, but it also connects to Yarde's childhood. Indigo blue was a color that the artist had first gravitated toward in his childhood lessons at the MFA; when he was facing what might have been the end of his career, the color took on a broader resonance that reconfirmed his connection to the spiritual influence of the dream world. He now recognized indigo as the medium traditionally used to dye Central African textiles and as the color of fabric used by hoodoo practitioners for wrapping *helping hands* that are designed to protect the well-being of the home.

In 2000 Yarde received a kidney transplant, by which point his work had changed forever. If *Mojo Hand* had signaled a shift from the historical reportage found in the work completed prior to his illness, his new projects continued to revel in a larger Diasporic history that fused personal history with cosmic questions, wrestling with magic, mortality, and the fragility of the human condition. As these works evolved, Yarde began to use double sheets of paper, sutured together, to form square planes. In *Ring Shout*, 2002 (figure 3), the quadrant formed by doubling the rectangular linear grid of *Mojo Hand* bends to encapsulate a circle within which the three key elements of mouths, hands, and shoes are marshaled. Three concentric registers radiate outward from a central grid of blue squares. The first register contains four open mouths placed at what appear to be the cardinal locations of north, south, east, and west. The mouths are in turn separated by twelve palm prints, three between each mouth, oriented in a coun-

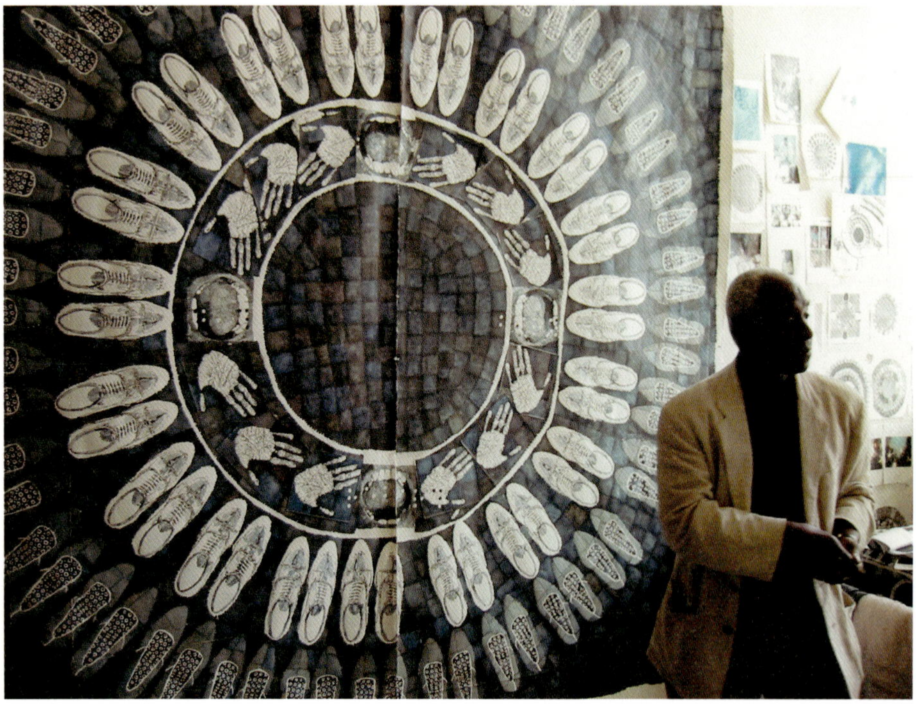

Figure 3.
The artist in his studio with *Ring Shout*, 2002.
Courtesy of the author.

terclockwise direction. The two outer registers are comprised of identical sets of mens and womens shoes, arranged in pairs, with their toes pointing inward.

The title of the piece refers to the ceremony of the *ring shout*, an African American folk ritual with roots in several Central West Africa traditions, including those of the Bantu, the Igbo and the Akan, the Yoruba, and most significantly the Kongo.[11] The ring shout is characterized by a counterclockwise circumlocution that visually expresses integrated beliefs of cosmic lifecycles. Like the hoodoo belief in the power of *mojo hands* to help their owners, the *ring shout* is another type African retention fomented in the southern United States.[12]

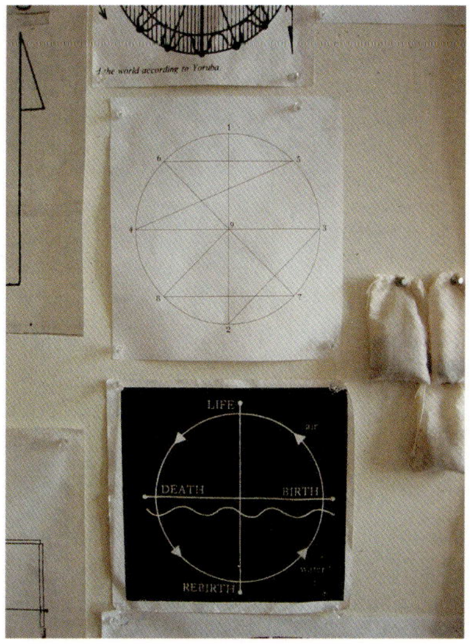


Figure 4.
Kikongo cosmogram, or *Tendwa Nza Kongo*, at the bottom, with related geometric drawing at the top, on the wall of the artist's studio, 2002.
Courtesy of the author.

During the antebellum period *ring ceremonies* held on plantations were often associated with magic and with ancestral life.[13] In *The Slave Community*, historian John Blassingame also cites the *ring shout* as one of the best examples of the syncretic merging of African and Christian religious practices. Drawing on nineteenth-century sources, Blassingame claims that the shouting, singing, and movement of the *ring shout* enabled slaves to release their dispair and to express their desires for freedom.[14] Historian Sterling Stuckey has subsequently argued that the advent of the ring shout in African American culture is best understood in its relation to the Kikongo cosmogram, or *Tendwa Nza Kongo* (figure 4).[15]

Representing the "four moments of the sun," the arrangement of a Greek cross surrounded by lines in *the Tendwa Nza Kongo* embraces cosmological movement of the sun's rising and setting as a cyclical analogue to the continuing relationship between the living and the dead.[16] It is a reminder of the permeable boundary between this world and the other, the melding of life, death, rebirth and birth.[17] This African cosmological perspective is reflected in the placement of the hands and mouths in the central register of *Ring Shout*, which also reference the design on the *Opon Ifa* divination trays (figure 5). *Opon Ifa* are used by the *babalawo*, the "father of ancient wisdom" who serves as a diviner in the Yoruba belief system of Nigeria and Benin, to help guide his supplicant through a difficult decision by making contact between the human world and the world of the spirits. Stuckey claims that cultural and religious tools like *Opon Ifa* divination trays, the *ring shout*, and circular imagery in general were an integral part of cultural and religious ceremonies that honored ancestors and asserted people's connection to the land in Africa. This tradition was continued in the closeknit slave communities of the an-

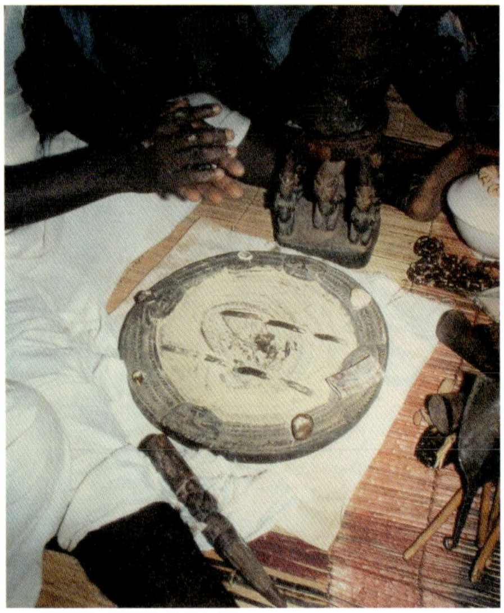

Figure 5.
Photograph of a Yoruba divination ceremony featuring an Opon Ifa, from the artist's studio, 2002. Courtesy of the author.

tebellum South; Sterling holds that "the use of the circle for religious purposes in slavery was so consistent and profound that one could argue that it was what gave form and meaning to black religion and art."[18]

Yarde's use of shoes references the *ring shout's* dancelike movement wherein men and women move in separate circles in a sort of shuffling motion, never lifting their feet from the ground, clapping and singing, as described by James Weldon Johnson in his autobiography:

When there was a "ring shout" the weird music and the sound of thudding feet set the silence of the night vibrating and throbbing with a vague terror. Many a time I woke suddenly and lay a long while strangely troubled by these sounds, the like of which my great-grandmother Sarah had heard as a child. The shouters, formed in a ring, men and women alternating, their bodies close together, moved round and round on shuffling feet that never left the floor. With the heel of the right foot they pounded out the fundamental beat of the dance and with their hands clapped out the varying rhythmical accents of the chant; for the music was, in fact, an African chant and the shout an African dance, whole pagan rite transplanted and adapted to Christian worship. Round and round the ring would go. One, two, three, four, five hours, the very monotony of sound and motion inducing an ecstatic frenzy.[19]

And yet, in *Ring Shout* the orientation of the shoes does not imply movement; rather they are shown paired up, attention focused on the central space of the composition, the space of divination. The importance of the cosmogram and the circle to Diasporic syncretic religion is witnessed in the use of Cuban firmas, palo mayombe drawings, flag altars, round sanctuaries, Brazilian pontos, and Haitian vévé.[20] In a similar way to Yarde's use of the ring shout to express community and healing rituals, artist Houston Conwill created the *The New Ring Shout* to commemorate the first graveyard for African Americans in New York City. One of several cosmograms completed by Conwill for public spaces, the piece is embedded in the floor of the General Services Administration building that was built on the site of the graveyard in 1992. Its presence allows visitors to reconnect with an ancestral site that incorporates "memories, histories, and spiritualities that are selectively or forcibly retained, reinvented, or erased."[21]

This desire to connect visually with the spirituality inherent in the divine circularity and spiritual patterns of West Central African healing traditions has been a way for Yarde to address his own personal crisis. His search for transcendence has also been a search for numerological significance in the fundamental structure of the grid, the 23rd psalm, and the 23 fundamental parts to the DNA molecule in *Mojo Hand*. And the doubling of the grid in *Ring Shout*, with its sets of three handprints (a continuation of the three pairs seen in the earlier work) surrounded by neatly mated shoes, continues this investigation into universal questions of structure and spirituality. Through his recent watercolors Yarde has conjured a powerful mixture of history and healing, one that has made dreams real and the real surreal.

## NOTES

1 A topical discussion of Yarde's working practice and an overview of his career can be found in Alona Horn, "Showing Vital Signs: The Watercolors of Richard Yarde." *American Visions*, February-March 1998.
2 Metcalf, a master watercolorist himself, upon learning that his young protégé would have to take time away from his studies to earn tuition money, gave the university administration a bold ultimatum: he threatened to resign from the faculty of the art department unless Yarde was awarded a scholarship. The administration relented and the young painter was able to complete his degree without interruption.
3 The potential for the bonds between artists and the dedication of teachers to their students that Yarde experienced at BU under Metcalf influenced his own teaching and personal relationships. Since the early 1970s Yarde has taught painting in a number of New England art departments, and for the last decade at the University of Massachusetts, Amherst. During this period his work was collected by over thirty museums including the Studio Museum in Harlem, the Museum of Fine Art, Boston, the National Museum of American Art, and the Metropolitan Museum of Art, New York.
4 For a discussion of Yarde's spiritual journey during his dialysis see Tamara Jeffries, "Going Under: Artists on the Healing Power of Art Making," *The International Review of African American Art* 16, no. 4 (2000), 2-15.
5 I use the term syncretic as an adjective describing "the developmental process of historical growth within a religion by accretion and coalescence of different and often orig. conflicting forms of belief and practice through the interaction with or supersession of other religions." *Webster's Third International Dictionary, Unabridged* (Online Version, 1999-2000 Bell & Howell Information and Learning Company).
6 *Webster's Third International Dictionary, Unabridged* (Online Version, 1999-2000 Bell & Howell Information and Learning Company).
7 Harry Middleton Hyatt, *Hoodoo—Conjuration—Witchcraft—Rootwork: Beliefs Accepted by Many Negroes and White Persons These Being Orally Recorded by Blacks and Whites.* (Washington: distributed by American University Bookstore, 1970), vol. 1, p. 519.
8 For a more complete discussion of *hands, hoodoo,* and *mojo* see Catherine Yronwode's online book, *Hoodoo In Theory And Practice: An Introduction to African-American Rootwork* and her *Lucky W Amulet Archive*, at www.luckymojo.com.
9 In *Mules and Men*, Zora Neale Hurston's record of the hoodoo practices and beliefs that were thriving in the 1930s, root doctor Luke Turner describes his grandmother the renowned hoodoo priestess Marie Laveau beginning a curse by placing her hands flat upon the table. Zora Neale Hurston, *Mules and Men* (Philadelphia: Lippincott Publishers, 1935), pp. 196-197.
10 For several Native American cultures, including the Inuit peoples of the Arctic Circle and those living further south along what is today the northwest coast of British Columbia and Washington State, the skeleton is also a traditional shamanic image. For these people the skeleton signifies that part of the shaman's body that would survive the impact of the elements long after he was dead. In this way the bones were the core of the shaman's power, emblematic of the second sight with which a magical community healer was ritually endowed.
11 Michael Gomez, *Exchanging our Country Marks: The Transformation of African Identities in the Colonial and Antebellum South* (Chapel Hill: The University of North Carolina Press, 1998), pp. 118, 135, 149.
12 Ibid., p. 250.
13 In a traditional story of how a group of enslaved Igbo people flew back to Africa from Ebo Landing, a location on St. Simons Island off the Georgia coast, the slaves flight was preceded by a ring dance which grew faster and faster until the slaves took flight. See Gomez, p. 118.

14 John Blassingame, *The Slave Community: Plantation Life in the Antebellum South* (New York: Oxford University Press, 1979), pp. 134-135.
15 For a full discussion of the Kongo cosmogram and its impact on Diasporic African visual culture, see the work of art historian Robert Farris Thompson, in particular *Flash of the Spirit: African and Afro-American Art and Philosophy* (New York: Random House, 1983), and *The Four Moments of the Sun: Kongo Art in Two Worlds* (Washington, D.C.: National Gallery of Art, 1981).
16 In addition to their impact on various ring ceremonies in West Central Africa and the southern United States, Kongo cosmograms have been found in material recently unearthed from slave cabins at archaeological sites including the "curer's cabin" at the Levi Jordan Plantation in Brazoria, Texas. See Kenneth L. Brown, "Material Culture and Community Structure: The Slave and Tenant Community at Levi Jordan's Plantation, 1848-1892," in *Working Toward Freedom: Slave Society and Domestic Economy in the American South*, edited by Jr. Larry E. Hudson (Rochester, NY: University of Rochester Press, 1995), pp. 95-118.
17 Sterling Stuckey, *Slave Culture: Nationalist Theory and the Foundations of Black America* (New York: Oxford University Press, 1987), pp. 8-99.
18 Ibid., p. 11.
19 James Weldon Johnson, *Along This Way: The Autobiography of James Weldon Johnson* (New York: Da Capo Press, 1973; reprint of 1933 edition), p. 22, as quoted in Robert L. Hall, "African Religious Retentions in Florida." in *Africanisms in American Culture*, edited by Joseph E. Holloway (Bloomington: Indiana University Press, 1990), p. 108.
20 For more on these see Robert Farris Thompson, *Face of the Gods: Art and Altars of Africa and the African Americas* (New York: Museum for African Art ; Munich: Prestel, 1993).
21 Andrea Frohne, "Commemorating the African Burial Ground in New York City: Spirituality of Space in Contemporary Art Works." *Ijele: Art eJournal of the African World* (2000). http://www.ijele.com/ijele/vol1.1/frohne.html.

# BIOGRAPHIES

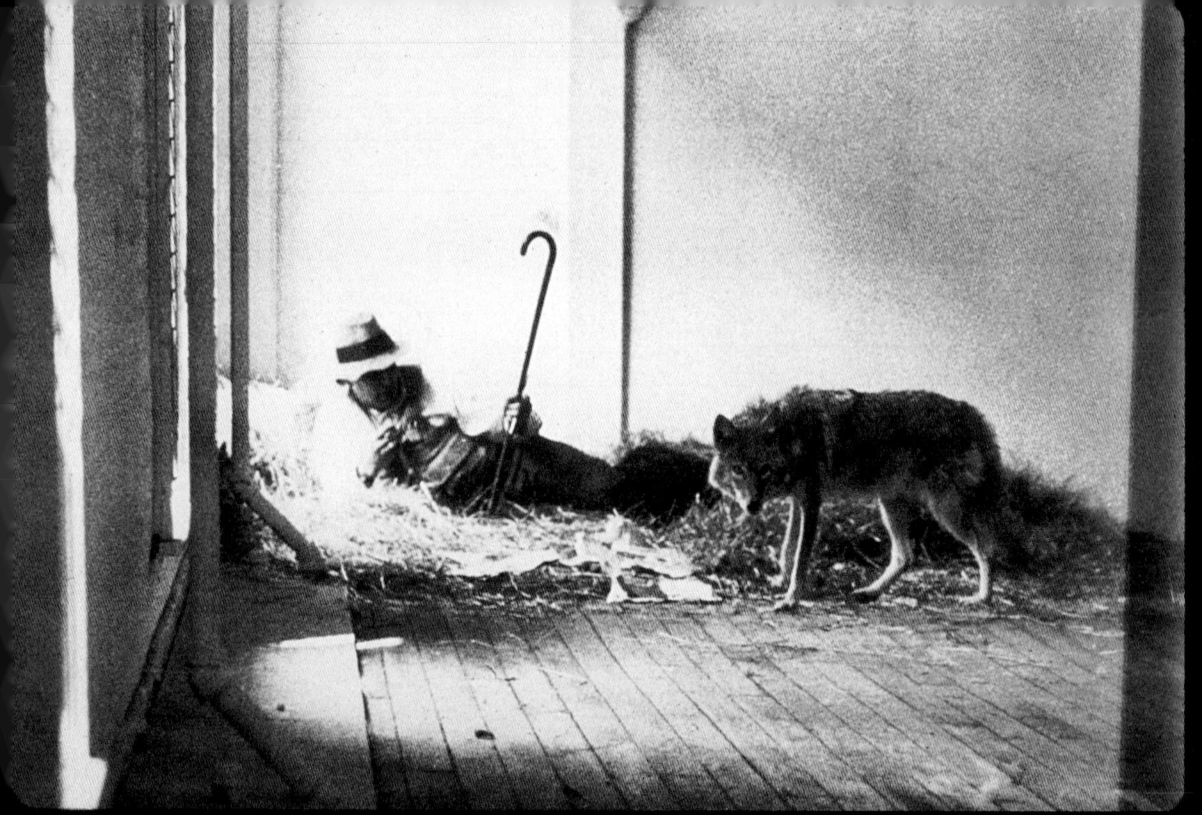
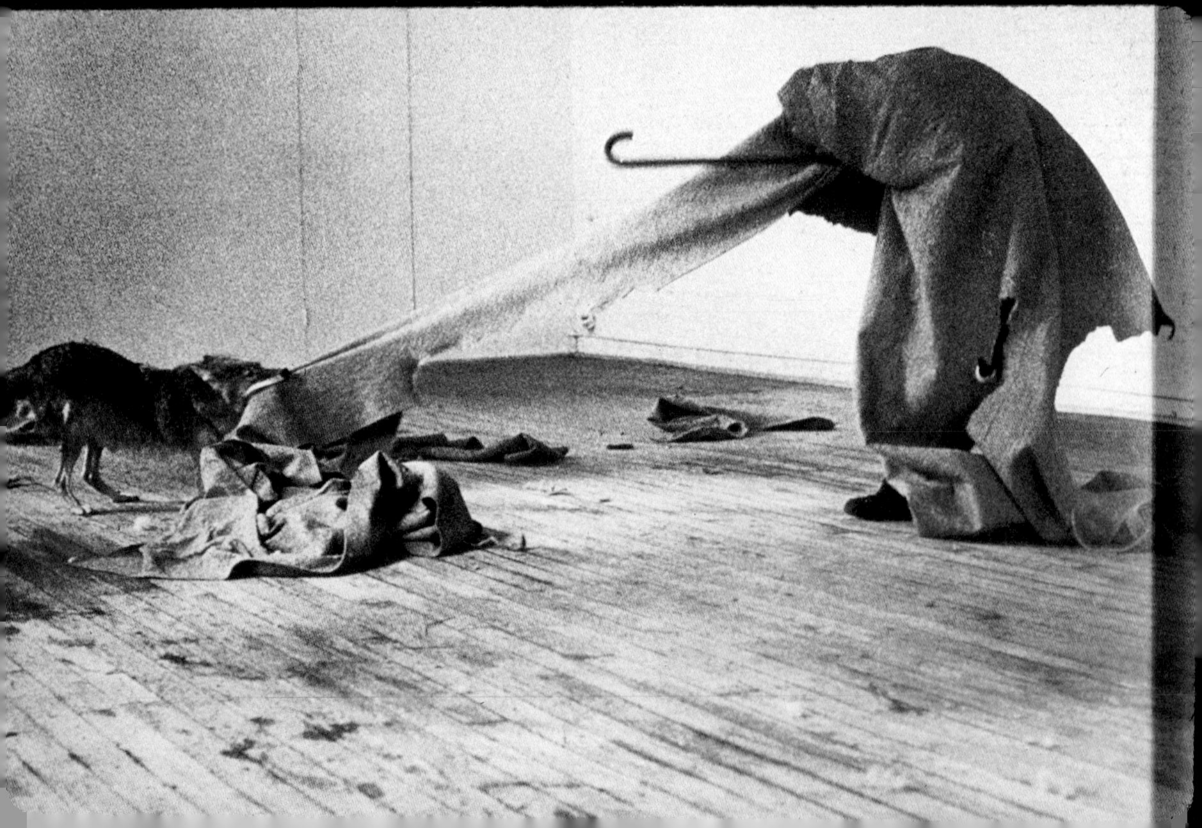

## JOSEPH BEUYS

Born in Krefeld, Germany, 1921. Died in Düsseldorf, Germany, 1986.

At once artist, teacher, political activist, theorist, therapist, and shaman, Joseph Beuys was one of the most important figures on the European artistic scene in the second half of the twentieth century. His essential contribution to modern art was to have elaborated an original system capable of redefining the creative act (with the "expanded concept of art" and of "social sculpture") and its ultimate purpose: nothing less than the transformation of society and humanity.

For Beuys, the role of the artist is to heal the ills of our ailing humanity: to treat the still raw moral wounds of postwar Germany; to cure Western man of the rationalism and materialism that are alienating him and stifling his intuition, preventing him from gaining access to the spiritual domain; and to restore his ruptured ties to nature.

Injury and malady are concretely evoked in his work by the frequent recourse to elements borrowed from the world of medicine: red cross, gauze, bandages (*Mädchen/Girl*, 1957), X-rays, metal utensils, and dressings. For instance, *Rückenstütze eines feingliedrigen Menschen (Hasentypus) aus dem 20. Jahrhundert n. Chr./Back support for a fine-limbed person (Hare-type) of the 20th century A.D.*, 1972 is a cast of a backbrace worn by the daughter of one of his artist friends.

What matters to Beuys more than the physical aspect of injury, however, is the moral aspect. Thus the evocation of trauma and suffering as cathartic elements plays an essential role in his work, starting with an (authentic or legendary?) traumatic episode from his own biography: when he served with the German air force during World War II, his plane was shot down in Crimea. He was found buried in snow by nomadic tribesmen, who took care of him: "They covered my body in fat to help it regenerate warmth and wrapped it in felt as an insulator to keep warmth in."[1]

This foundational event structures the symbolism in Beuys's work through the idea of death and resurrection (which is central to a number of his actions, in particular his first individual performance, *Der Chief/The Chief*, 1964, during which he rolled himself up in a felt blanket and remained immobilized on the ground for eight hours), and especially through the use of those two key materials (fat and felt), which became emblematic of his work.

Quite apart from the autobiographical reference, felt and fat figure in a more general sense in Beuys's "Theory of Sculpture," which was elaborated around two key notions, Chaos (associated with heat and formlessness) and Order (associated with cold, with solidified form), and around the transformation from one state to the other. Fat and honey, which liquefy under the action of heat, are the most explicit examples of this. All the materials that Beuys uses, generally common or elementary, are notable for their particular reaction to energy, which they

*left page:*
Joseph Beuys,
photograph of *Coyote: I Like America and America Likes Me*,
1974,
René Block Gallery,
New York

may generate (electrical batteries), store (the insulating nature of felt), or transmit (copper and iron as conductors).

The energy which circulates in a real or symbolic sense in his devices is supposed to liberate energies buried in the unconscious of the spectator, resulting in an inner transformation, a necessary step toward a transformation of society. Assuming the role of shaman, or spiritual guide, Beuys showed the way and subjected himself to this process of transformation in any number of actions that he performed between 1963 and 1985.

One of the most fascinating of these, *Coyote: I Like America and America Likes Me*, was presented as therapy for America: "I believe I made contact with the psychological trauma point of the United States' energy constellation: the whole American trauma with the Indian, the Red man." Refusing to enter into contact with any "representative" of America other than the coyote, an animal venerated by the Indians, Beuys was wrapped in a felt blanket that covered his face when he arrived at the airport in New York, and he was then transported in an ambulance to the René Block gallery, where the animal was waiting for him. Equipped with symbolic objects (copper cane, triangle, felt cover, flashlight, gloves), Beuys assumed a series of postures and performed various ritual gestures at regular intervals in order to channel the animal's chaotic energy and harmonize its relation to him. Fifty copies of *The Wall Street Journal*, symbolizing urban civilization (and, more specifically, capitalism), were delivered each day and used as litter for the coyote. After three days of wordless "dialogue," the coyote's spiritual authority was restored, and Beuys returned to Europe in the same way that he arrived.

The central idea governing Beuys's activities was that "every man is an artist": every man has the ability to participate in the transformation, the "shaping," of his economic, juridical, social, and political environment. All life situations and human activities are therefore potential contexts of "creation" in this expanded sense. By this reasoning, Beuys's works (drawings, sculptures, installations) should be seen as equivalents of his actions in the political and social realms: organization of the direct democracy movement (1971), campaign on behalf of the Green Party (1982), founding of the Free International University (1982), etc.

In one of his last works, *7000 Eichen/7000 Oaks*, Beuys planned to plant seven thousand oak trees (each accompanied by a prism-shaped balsamic stone) in the city of Kassel. Begun by Beuys in 1982, the effort was carried on by local residents and associations, which played an active part in planting the trees. The work, completed after Beuys's death by his son for Documenta 8 (1987), brings together Beuys's ecological, symbolic, and social concerns in a magisterial way and stands, outside the institutions of the world of art, as a lasting visible monument to the concept of "social sculpture."

SM

1 Quoted in Caroline Tisdall, *Joseph Beuys* (New York: The Solomon R. Guggenheim Museum, 1979), p. 17.

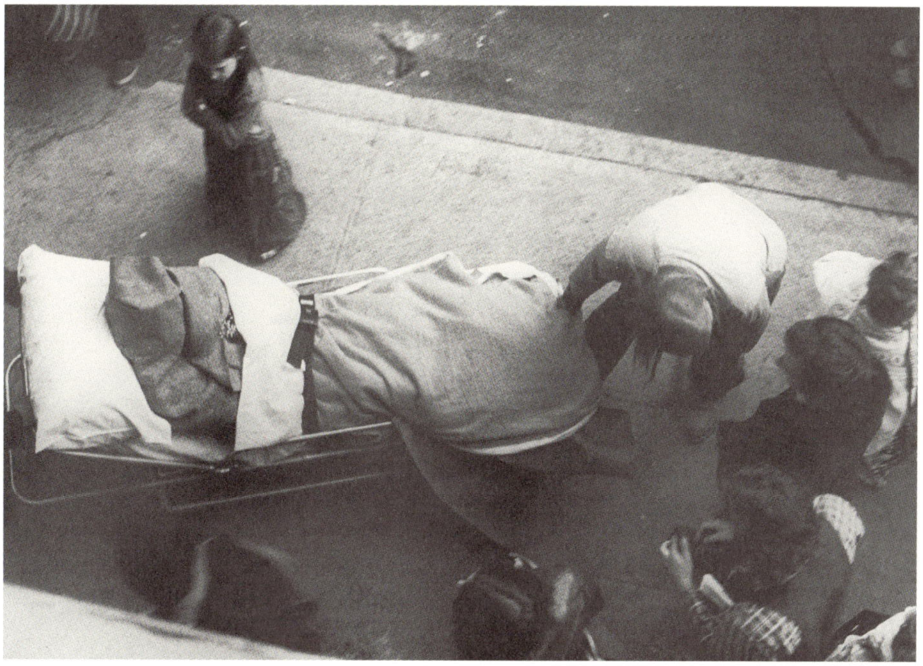

Joseph Beuys,
photograph of *Coyote: I Like America and America Likes Me*,
1974,
René Block Gallery,
New York

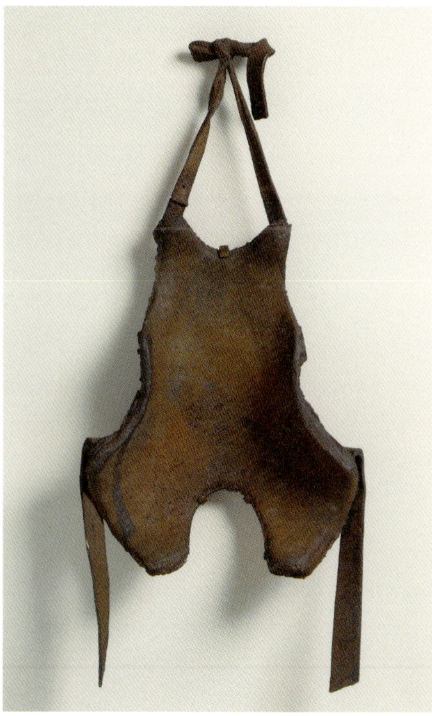

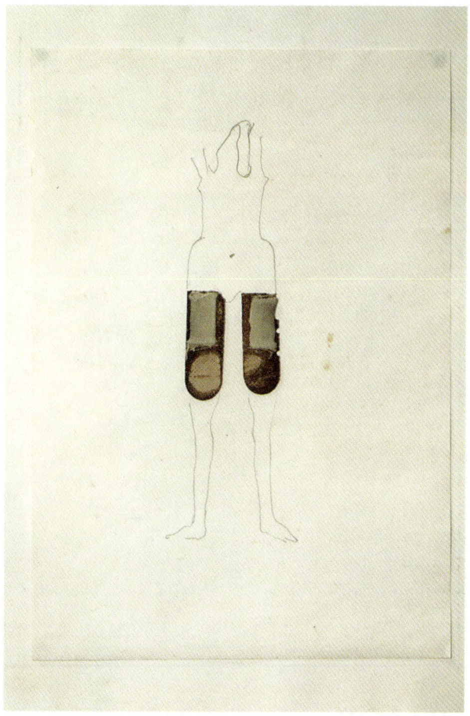

*left:*
Joseph Beuys,
*Back Support for a Fine-Limbed Person (Hare Type) of the 20th Century A.D., 1972.*
Collection of the Busch-Reisinger Museum,
Harvard University Art Museums,
The Willy and Charlotte Reber Collection,
Patrons of the Busch-Reisinger Museum Fund.

*right:*
Joseph Beuys,
*Mädchen (Girl),*
1957.
Collection of Museum Schloss Moyland

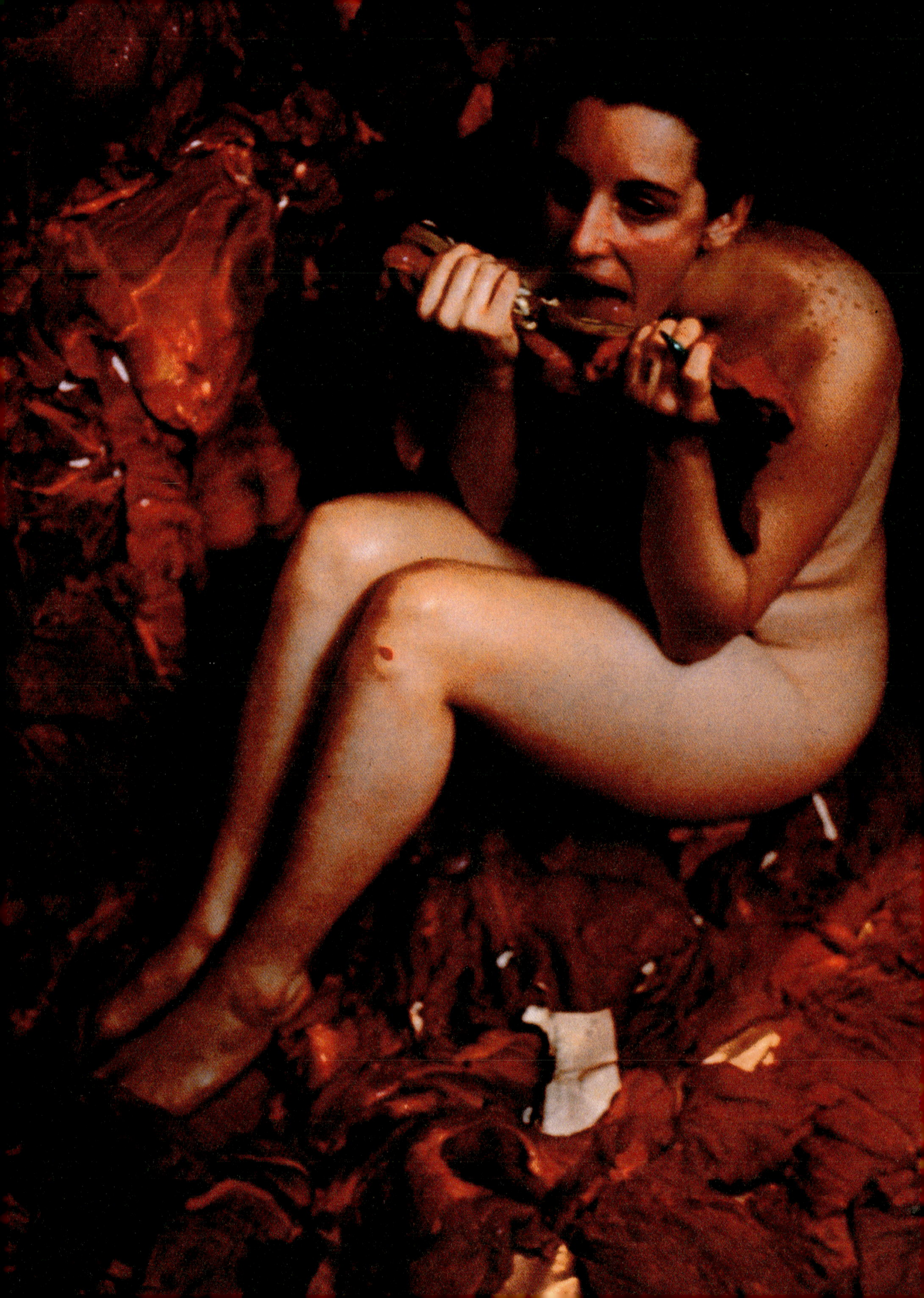

## TANIA BRUGUERA

Born in Havana, Cuba, 1968. Lives in Havana

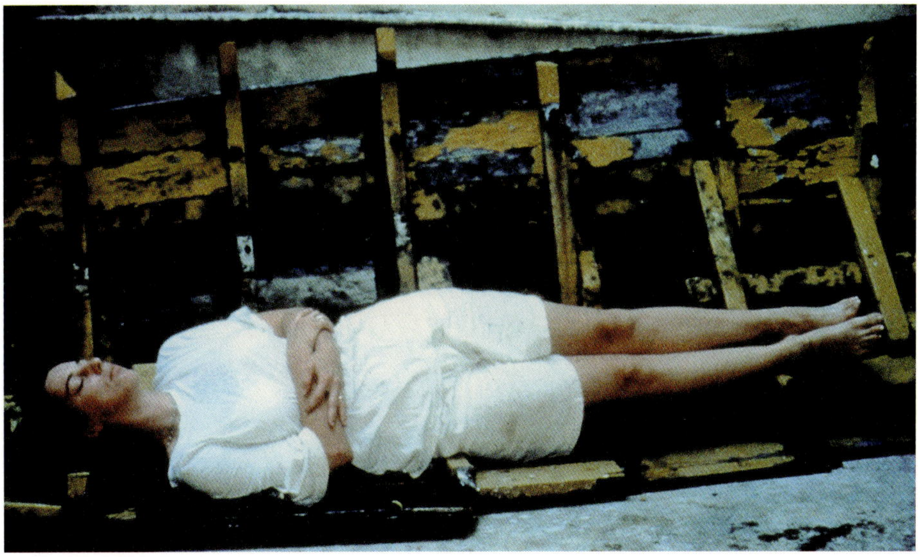

Tania Bruguera, *Miedo (Fear)*, 1994

At the age of 34, Tania Bruguera is one of the best-known Cuban artists of her generation. Since her inclusion in Havana's Eleventh Biennale in 1997, her work has appeared in numerous international exhibitions and installations (including the Biennales of contemporary art in São Paulo, Johannesburg, Santa Fe, Venice, Kwangju, Documenta, etc.).

Despite her frequent travel, Tania Bruguera remains deeply attached to Cuba. In contrast to many of her compatriots (the vast majority of the artists of the so-called "generation 80" went into exile in the nineties), she chose to continue living and working on the island and to place the experience of the Cuban people—her country's very distinctive social, political, religious, and cultural reality—at the heart of her work.

Convinced that art must be an experience, that it must be lived if it is to achieve its full communicative power, she gives priority to installations and performances: "I realized that performance was the best way for me to deal with social and political issues—it has the immediacy of need, the intensity of life, and the freedom of the ephemeral. It was also the best way to find the human element in these issues, by which people were truly affected and changed in the process."[1]

Bruguera's performances—in a sense ceremonies of collective catharsis in which she officiates—approach the most sensitive themes of Cuban reality in an allegorical manner: emigration, relations between the individual and the government, censorship, the illusion of utopia, guilt, memory, submission, isolation, and rumor.

*left page:*
Tania Bruguera, *Cuerpo del silencio (Body of Silence)*, 1998

Bruguera began her reflection on emigration, one of the most important themes in her art, with her work on the oeuvre of the Cuban-born American

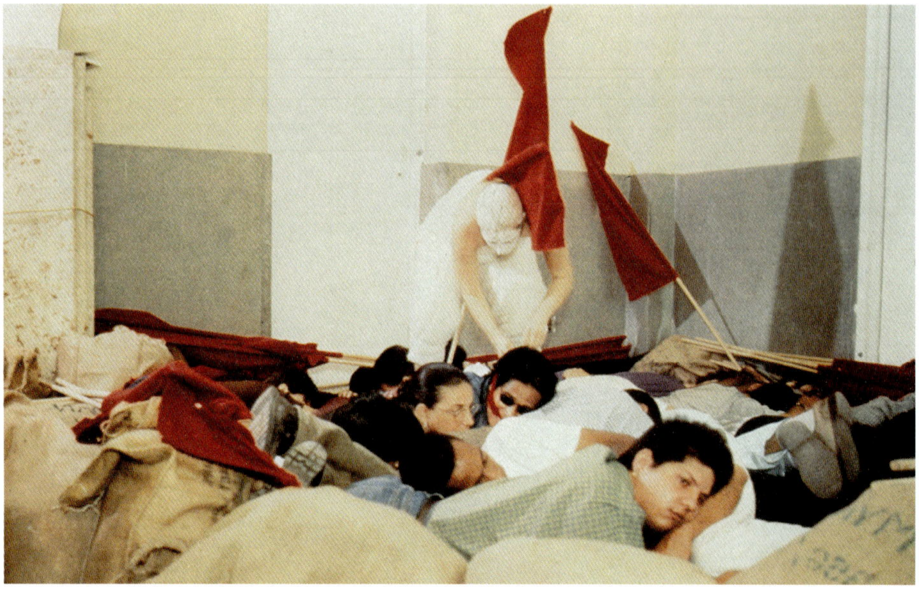

Tania Bruguera, Cabeza Abajo (Head Down), 1997

artist Ana Mendieta. By exhibiting her "re-creations" of Mendieta's works in 1992 (*Homenaje a Ana Mendieta/Tribute to Ana Mendieta*), she overcame the physical disappearance of the artist (who died in 1985) by creating the illusion of a return to the land of her birth while at the same time overcoming her symbolic disappearance by rehabilitating her memory within an official history from which all exiles were deliberately excluded. *Memoria de la postguerra/Memory of the Postwar* (1994), a work that takes the form of an alternative newspaper collecting contributions from Cuban artists, critics, and writers either living in Cuba or in exile (and which, after being censored by the authorities following the appearance of the second issue, has recently been revived in oral form), responds to the same need to unite two communities, to create a space for dialogue and collective reflection, for mental reconstruction of the territory beyond Cuba's borders. While prototypes of machines for learning how to fly (*Dédalo o el imperio de salvación/Daedalus or the Empire of Salvation*, 1995) suggest the *idea* of flight and escape rather than the actual act, performances such as *Tabla de salvación/Table of Salvation* (1994) and *Miedo/Fear* (1995) explicitly refer to the experience of the *balseros*, or would-be exiles who attempt to reach Florida in makeshift vessels.

Bruguera frequently uses dramatic stagings based on ritual and repetition in which she generally appears naked and works with organic materials such as earth, wood, cotton, hair, skin, bones, and fat. In *El peso de la culpa/The Burden of Guilt* (first performed in Cuba in 1997 and repeated several times since then)—one of her most poignant performances by virtue of both its symbolic content and its "visceral" aspect—the artist kneels in front of a funeral banner made of tufts of human hair and narrow strips of cloth (*Estadistica/Statistics*, 1996), with the carcass of a lamb hanging from her neck as both a protective shield and symbol of submission. Reviving the legendary sacrifice of the native Indians in the Spanish conquest of Cuba, she ritually forms pellets of earth and muddy water, which she then swallows, literally ingesting her own land. Her work paints a complex picture of the relation between guilt and responsibility: "The punishment is for being submissive, but that passivity is also a way to survive, and that kind of salvation is a slow death."[2]

Bruguera's aspiration to share the "realization" of her works, whether in terms of execution as such (other artists, friends, and neighbors contributed to the execution of *Estadistica* by donating their hair or participating in the lengthy chore of sewing) or of performance (*Ingeniero de almas* [Souls Engineer], Poggibonsi, 2000), has developed into a very radical posture. In her series *Behaviour Art: Translations*,[3] the videos of which are being shown at the ICA, she is no longer the author of her performances: she "transmits" them orally to neophytes who are free to interpret the subject and the artist's explanations from their own point of view and in whatever medium suits them. Realized in cities in which the artist has resided (Delhi, London, Lima), these "translations" shift the focus from the action as such to the conditions under which it is realized. This enables Bruguera to contextualize her themes in a new way and to explore the evolution of her work outside its original context: new territory, new language, new media. She thus addresses the paradox of how to be universal while remaining insular.

SM

## NOTES

1 "Tania Bruguera, Freedom of the Ephemeral," interview by Jens Hoffmann in *Flash Art International*, July-September 2001.

2 "Tania Bruguera in conversation with Octavio Zaya," *Cuba, Maps of Desire* (Vienna: Kunsthalle, 1999).

3 "Translations" being Bruguera's substitute for "performance," which is also closely associated with the performing arts.

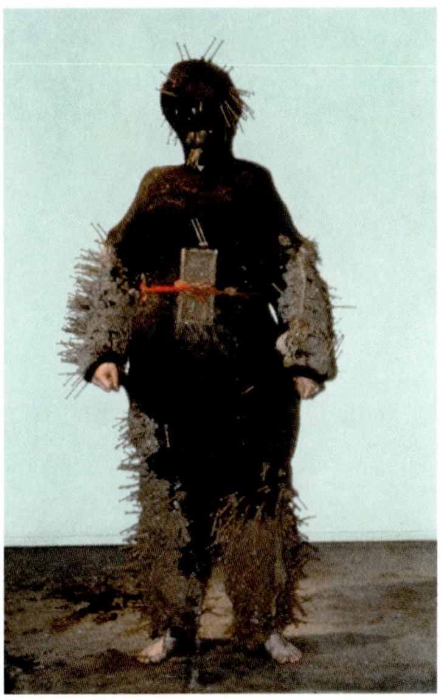

Tania Bruguera, *Destierro (Displacement)*, 1998–99

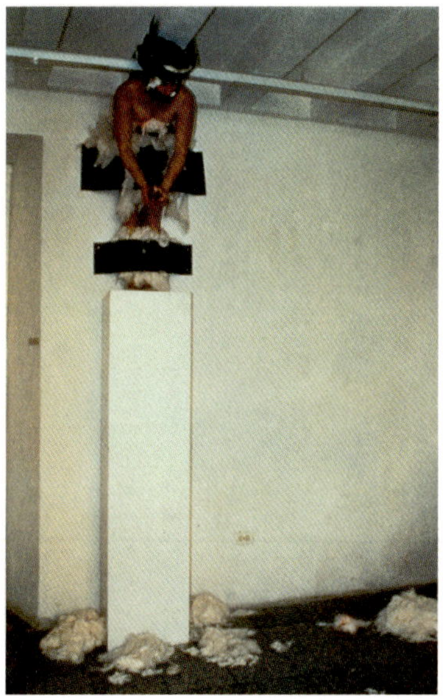

Tania Bruguera, *Estudio de taller (Studio study)*, 1996

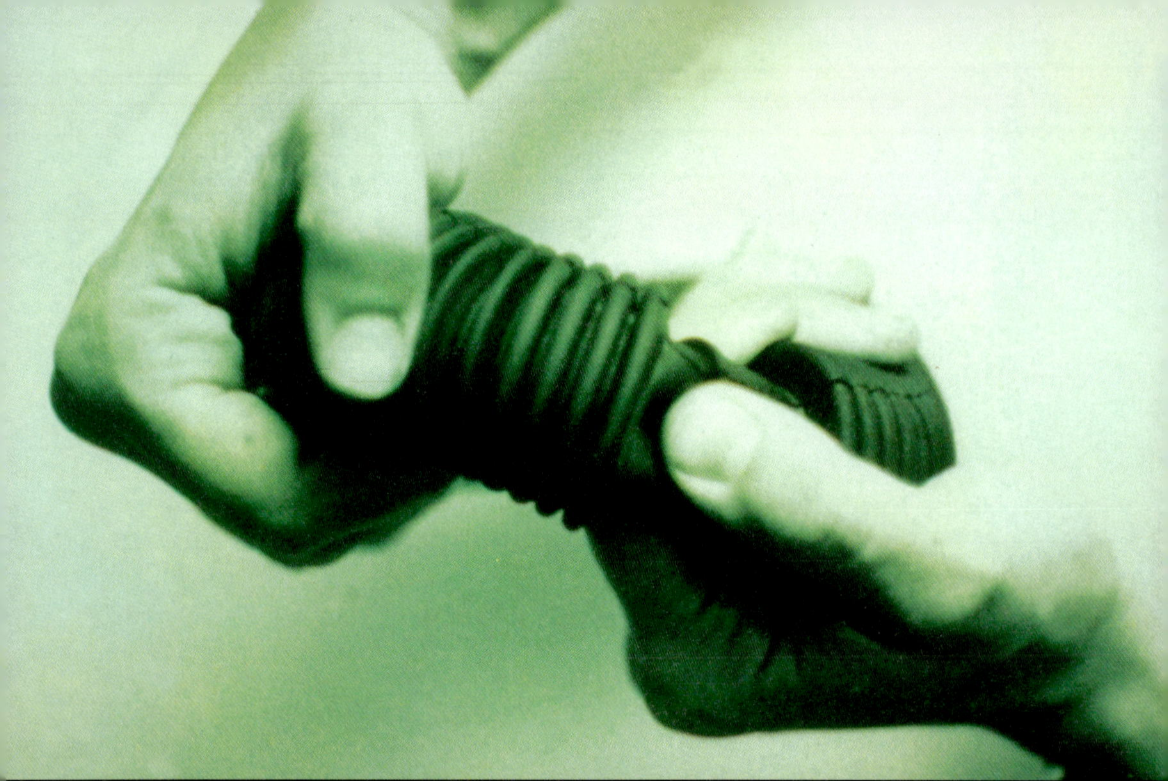

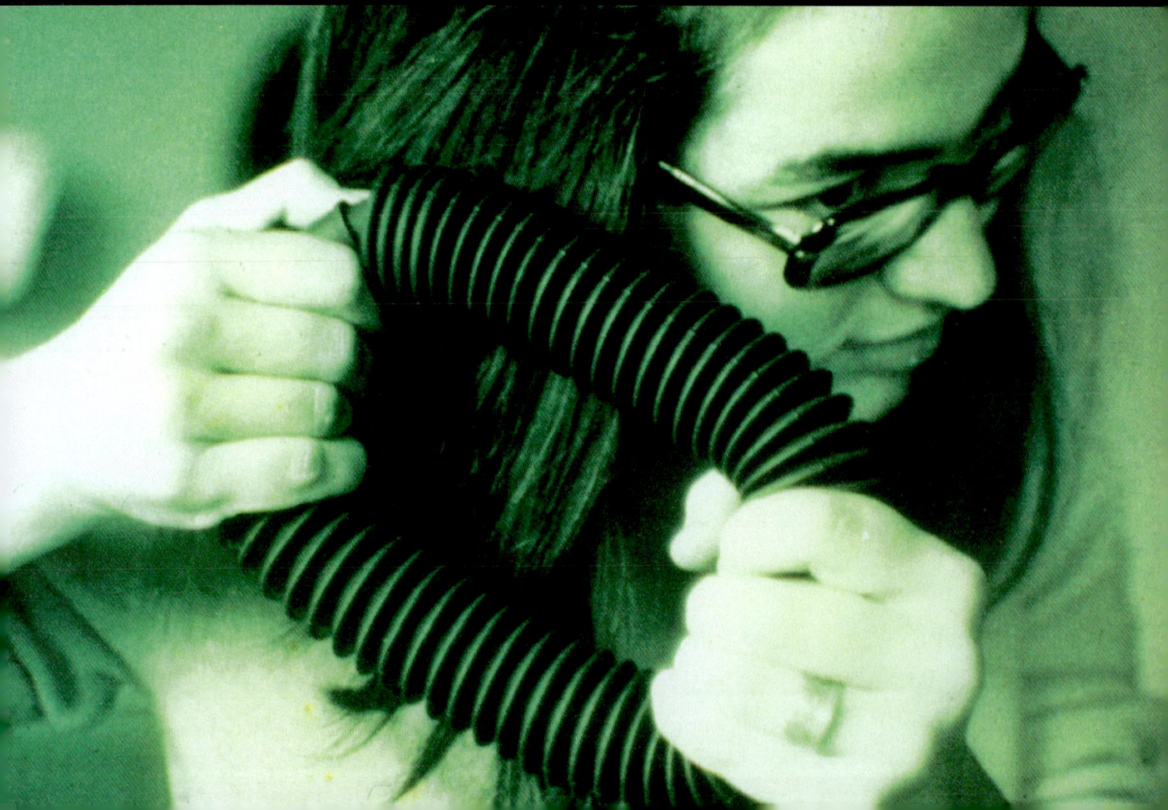

## LYGIA CLARK

Born in Belo Horizonte, Brazil, 1920. Died in Rio de Janeiro, 1988.

From its beginnings as a student of the landscape architect Roberto Burle Marx in Rio, Lygia Clark's development as an artist—from constructivist painter to therapeutic art practitioner—might confound conventional expectations of artistic advancement and our desire for logical progression within a career. Major shifts in practice are generally viewed with suspicion, in particular when they involve a movement away from abstraction toward a representational or figurative practice—think of Picasso's famous *retour à l'ordre* or Francis Picabia and Philip Guston's reversals—which is generally interpreted as a move from the experimental to the reactionary. Although Clark's work became in many ways increasingly figurative during her life, it was by no means a conservative return to the body. Rather, she posited a way of thinking *through* the figure or body toward a new conception of artistic communication. Indeed, Clark's very conception of the figure was itself a radical, new way of both conceiving and experiencing the body.

At the outset of her career, however, Clark's involvement was central to the Rio-based Brazilian constructivist movement. This association of artists, *Grupo Frente*, included Lygia Pape, Hélio Oiticica, and Ivan Serpa among others and was championed by the critic Mário Pedrosa. Their nonfigurative work was exhibited widely in the 1950s and became part of the rapid modernization experienced in Brazil that included such major architectural projects as Oscar Niemayer's city plan for Brasília. Although Clark's early abstract painting—influenced by her teachers Roberto Burle Marx and Fernand Léger—conforms to a constructivist conception of nonobjective art, in 1960 she began to produce three-dimensional works that required audience manipulation. Her *Bichos/Animals* are metal, articulated sculptures that can be arranged into a variety of forms. Clark's interest in architecture at this time (she had worked briefly with Niemayer and was well informed on contemporary architectural practice) was manifest in the planar forms of the *Bichos* that mimicked the type of architectural references that had appeared in her paintings but in three-dimensional form. Clark's perception of architecture as comparable to a body that houses man is anthropomorphized in the *Bichos* to suggest a protective receptacle akin to the body.

The manipulation of the *Bichos,* however, proved to be the key component of this work and led Clark to further theorize this participation as an open-ended process more akin to a "proposition" than to a finished artwork. The objects that she started to make subsequently have a highly provisional and experimental form—from the simple pebble placed on an air-filled plastic bag of *Pedra e ar/Stone and Air* to the rubber tubing of *Respire omigo/Breathe with Me.* These

*left page:*
Lygia Clark,
*Respire Comigo,*
1966

works were made to be touched, moved, and experienced by the audience as objects with inherent qualities suggestive of the major functions of the body: breathing, movement, birth, and so on. Clark abstracts these physical traits in order that the viewer can experience them as sensorial phenomena related to an interior experience but presented as an exterior event. Titled collectively *Nostalgia del cuerpo/Nostalgia of the Body*, the works propose a refamiliarization of the audience with their internal selves—re-presenting a knowledge that has been lost through modern existence.

Clark's investigation of architecture as a metaphor for the body undergoes a reversal in her subsequent series, *La casa es el cuerpo/The House Is the Body* whereby the body is conceived as architecture, or as the site of experience. Increasingly focused on questioning the boundaries and liminalities of the internal/external, mind/body, male/female, Clark develops a series of masks and clothing that explicitly contort the viewers' experience of these supposed dichotomies. Many of these works involve the manipulation of sight such that the viewer/participant is forced to rely on alternative senses and, potentially, to experience a new mind-body totality. These experiments were transformed into group events in the 1970s, during which time Clark worked closely with students at the Sorbonne in Paris, in a series titled *Fantasmática del cuerpo/The Phantasmagoria of the Body*. Rather than individual subjects manipulating objects or clothing, Clark devises collective works in which all participants are involved (there are no observers) and the artist's role is reduced to that of facilitator rather than sole creator.

During this transition from constructivist painting to collaborative works, Clark radically reimagines the roles of artist, audience, and artwork. This reconfiguration challenged the utopian, universalist ideals of her early work and involved the establishment of a philosophy that emphasized individual transformation—psychological as well as experiential. The final development in Clark's work resulted in the artist's fusion of the roles of doctor, or as she described herself, "researcher," and artist. *Estructuracíon del self/The Structuring of the Self*, Clark's title for her explicitly therapeutic practice of the 1980s, involved many of the early objects and masks that had appeared in her work in the previous decades. These materials and nigh-talismanic objects were manipulated by Clark in private "sessions" that enabled the patient/participant to reintegrate what had become an urbanized and desensitized "body of parts." Part psychotherapy, part ritual, Clark thought of this work as nothing less than a "structuring of the self," a desire no less ambitious than the universalist claims of constructivism, but one arrived at after many years of intense theoretical writing, artistic experimentation, and personal exploration.

JM

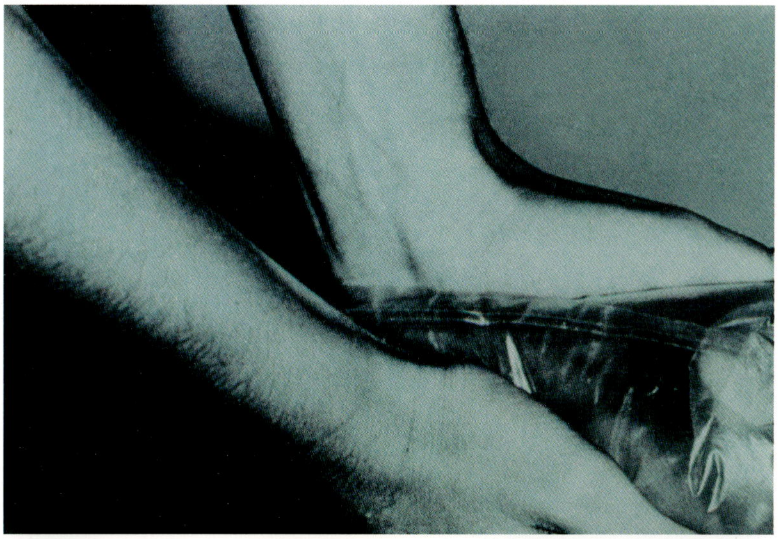

Lygia Clark,
*Pedra e Ar*,
1966

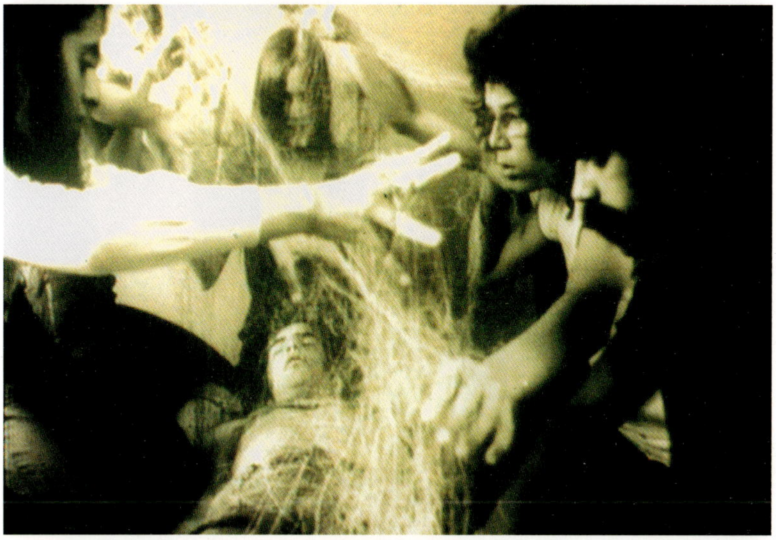

Lygia Clark,
*Baba antropofágica*,
1973

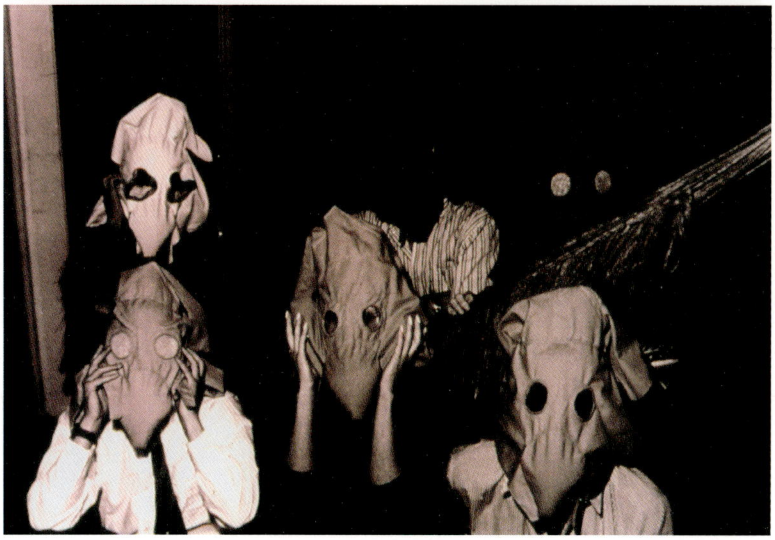

Lygia Clark,
*Mascara sensorais*,
1967

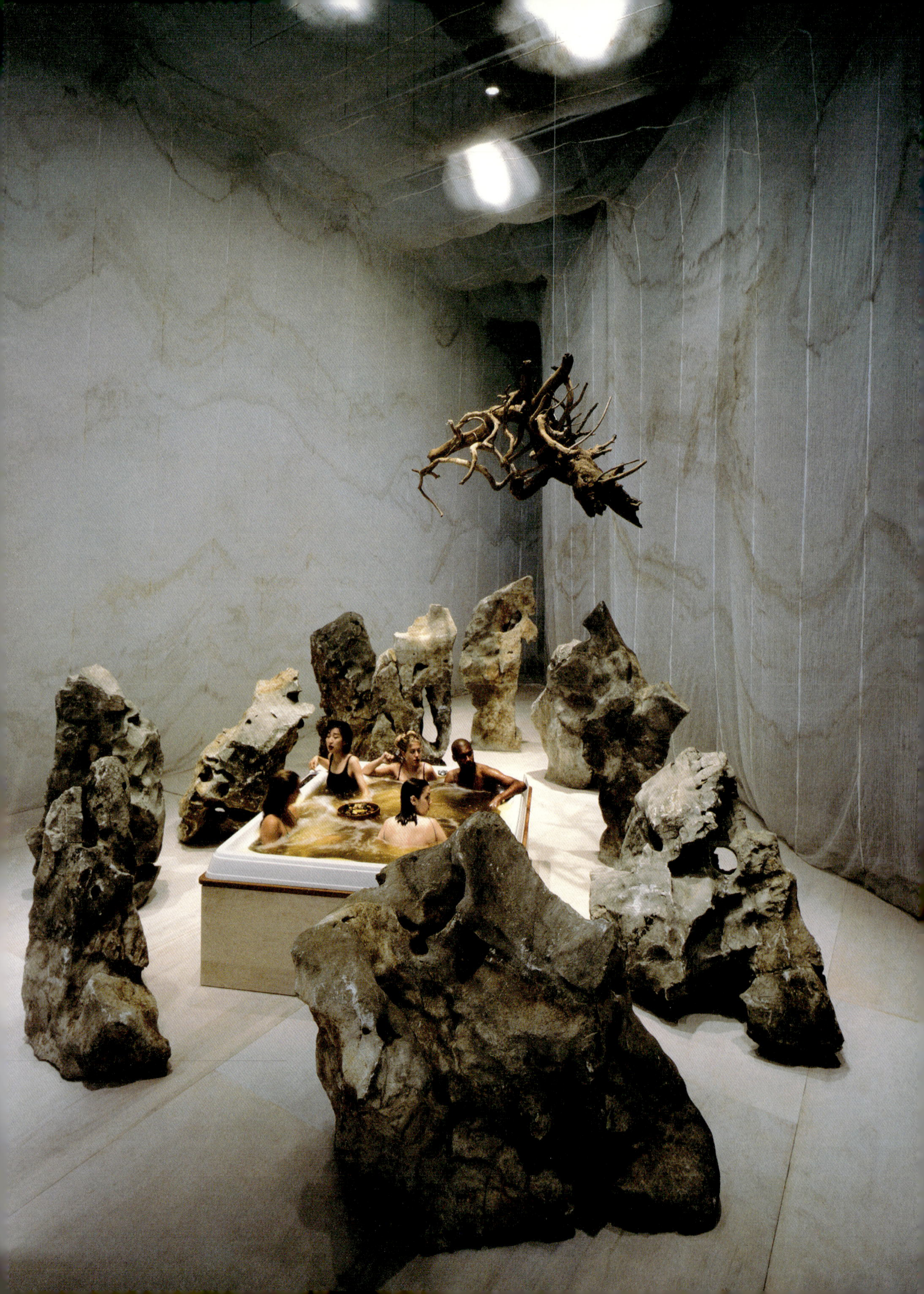

## CAI GUO-QIANG

Born in Quanzhou, Fujian Province, China, 1957. Lives in New York City.

Cai Guo-Qiang could be considered the quintessential, global contemporary artist—circling the world presenting his ambitious artworks, which, like Cai, are wide-ranging and peripatetic. Over the past twenty years, he has produced paintings, photographs, sculptures, installations, large-scale land art, and performance art—expanding the definition and understanding of these art forms in the process. Similarly, the themes and issues that his works touch upon have been diverse and provocative, including cultural politics, originality and authenticity, and the transformative, healing nature of art.

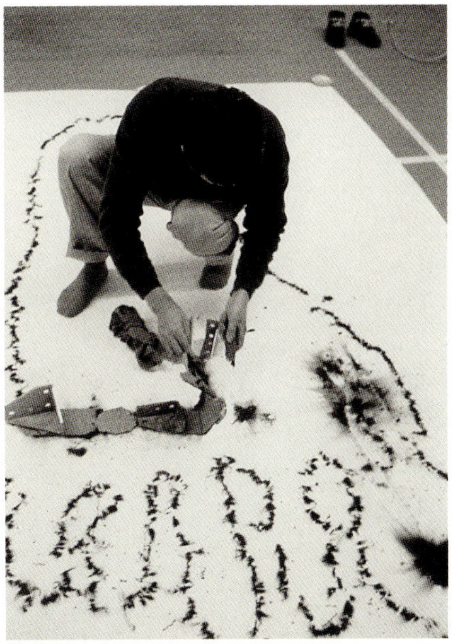

Cai Guo-Qiang, *A cure when ill, a supplement when healthy,* 1997, Installation at Museum of Contemporary Art, Chicago

Cai is perhaps most known for his gunpowder drawings and the large-scale earthworks that grew out of them. In the mid 1980s he began experimenting with gunpowder and firecrackers as "paint" on paper. While Cai's mastery of the technique allows him to design the gunpowder drawings' composition and imagery, his interest in the process stems more from the *lack* of control involved and the prevailing element of chance. He traces his initial attraction to the distinctive technique to his experiences as an artist living in China: "This was a release from the repression and pressure I felt around me. It was also an attempt to distance myself from traditional Chinese art, which is very much concerned with controlled form."[1]

Using his sketchbooks of gunpowder drawings as blueprints, in 1989 Cai envisioned a series of monumental events called *Projects for Extraterrestrials,* a series of large-scale, highly controlled outdoor explosions. While some of the *Projects* will probably only exist in drawings (for *Tectonic Plate Movement: Project for Extraterrestrials* N° 22, Cai suggests: "An explosion is set up next to a museum in an attempt to move the building")[2], Cai has realized over thirty *Projects* in locations around the world. These have included the extension of the Great Wall in China by 10,000 meters using gunpowder, the flight of a flaming silk dragon kite over Humlebaek, Denmark, and the explosive parting of a channel in Stockholm, Sweden. Each *Project* is unique and site specific, layered in symbolism and complex in social, cultural, and political meaning. Yet this aspect of the work relates to how *humans* understand the *Projects,* while Cai also

*left page:*
Cai Guo-Qiang, *Cultural Melting Bath: Project for the 20th Century,* 1997, Installation at Queens Museum of Art, New York

addresses a more otherworldly audience. As the name suggests, the series attempts to create a dialogue between the earth and the universe and its potential inhabitants. The *Projects*, although created *by* humans, are essentially made for those *outside* of this planet. When imagined on this universal scale, Cai's potentially overwhelming, dauntingly massive works become smaller, more humbling experiences.

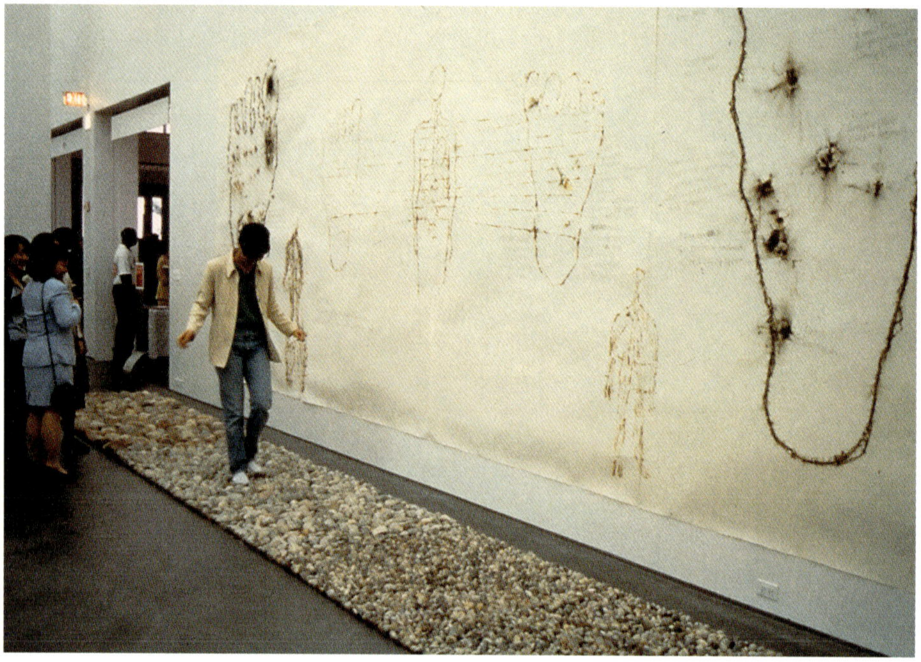

Cai Guo-Qiang, *A cure when ill, a supplement when healthy*, 1997, Installation at Museum of Contemporary Art, Chicago

Some critics have noted that when Cai moved to the United States from Japan in 1995, his work returned from the celestial realm to more earthly concerns.[3] While continuing his interest in the artistic process and intense viewer experience, many of his museum installations have focused on the involvement of the viewer, not as a passive spectator, but as an essential element in the completion of the artwork. *Cultural Melting Bath: Project for the 20th Century*, exhibited at the Queens Museum of Art, New York in 1997, included nine taihu limestone rocks, which are normally found in traditional Chinese gardens. These were arranged around a Jacuzzi that viewers were invited to sit in; a net surrounded the gallery, filled with live birds. The work was intended to be therapeutic and transformative physically, as well as (inter)personally. The rocks were placed to create the optimal space for the flow of one's chi, or vital energy, and the tub was infused with herbs for the skin. Beyond these bodily transformations, Cai enjoyed the "friction" produced between people of different cultures and backgrounds when encountering each other in the intimate space of a whirlpool; the work becomes a literal melting pot in the American city that most exemplifies the phrase.[4]

Cai's *A cure when ill, a supplement when healthy* includes a path of different-sized rocks that viewers walk over barefoot; the adjacent wall displays a gunpowder drawing diagramming the principles of reflexology. The stones lead to a vending machine where viewers can purchase herbal drinks for various ailments. Like *Cultural Melting Bath, A cure when ill* requires the visitors to "perform" the sculpture; the work is only completed when the viewer interacts with the piece, hopefully resulting in a healing, beneficial experience. It is not the art itself that "heals," but instead the therapeutic possibilities are unlocked by the viewer's willingness to participate in the piece. Whether in his large explosive works in outdoor settings or the installations he makes for museum visitors, Cai Guo-Qiang's work speaks directly to viewers, both human and extraterrestrial, through the generation of meaningful experiences, dialogue, and visual beauty.

EM

1 Cai Guo-Qiang, "Octavio Zaya in conversation with Cai Guo-Qiang," *Cai Guo-Qiang* (London: Phaidon Press Limited, 2002), p. 13.
2 Fei Dawei, Cai Guo-Qiang, and Andrei Ujica, *Cai Guo-Qiang* (London: Thames & Hudson, 2000), p. 141.
3 *Cai Guo-Qiang*, p. 22.
4 *Cai Guo-Qiang*, p. 28.

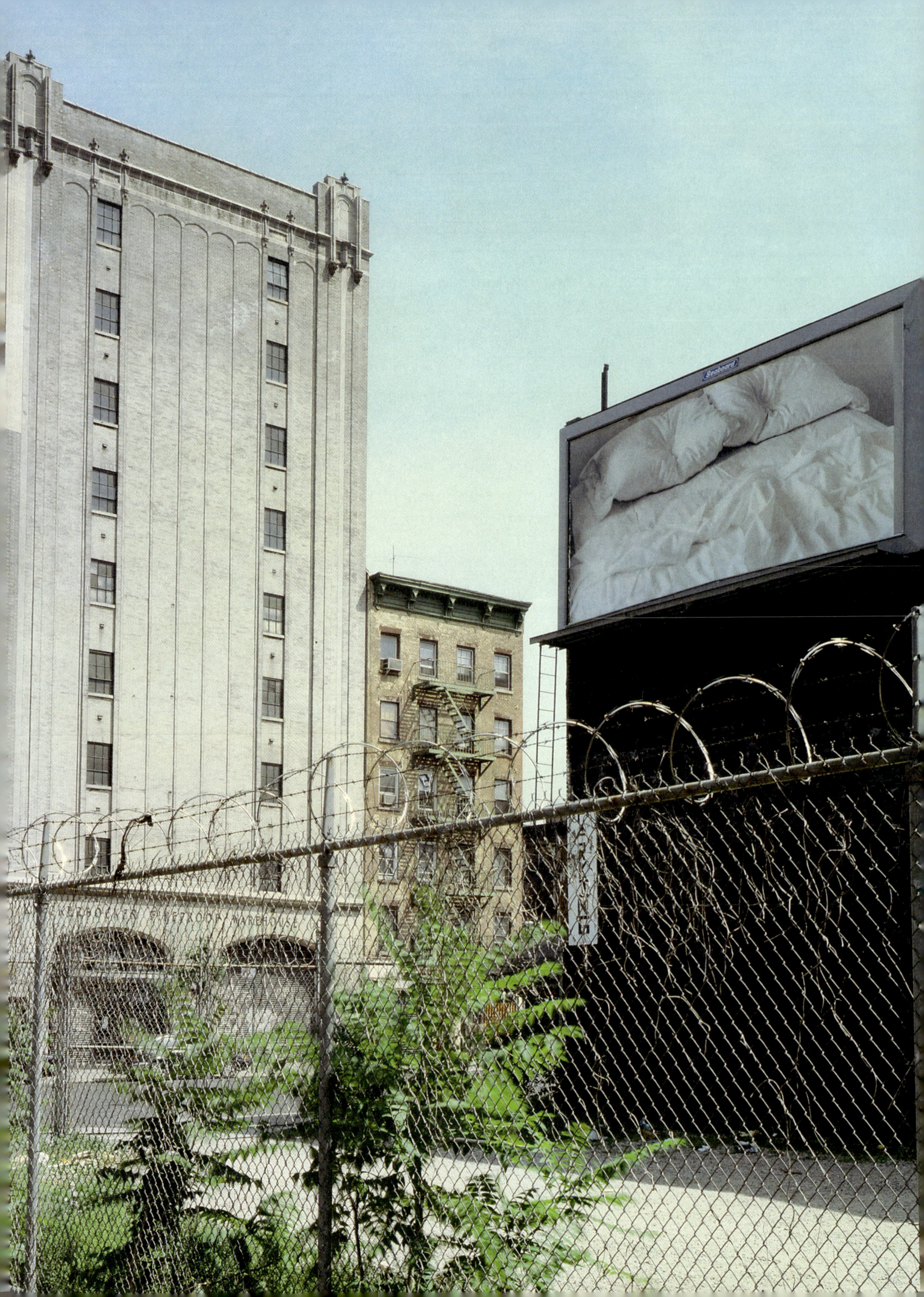
WAREHOUSE

## FELIX GONZALEZ-TORRES

Born in Guáimaro, Cuba, 1957. Died in Miami, Florida, 1996.

In 1992, the five boroughs of New York City were peppered with twenty-four identical billboards. The image on each was an empty double bed, the pillows still holding the imprint of once-resting bodies, the pristine sheets slightly wrinkled. The billboards, an untitled work by Felix Gonzalez-Torres, exemplify the artist's concerns—the blurred lines between the private and the public and the conflation of the personal with the political. The work could be seen as a public act of mourning for the artist's lover, who died the year before from AIDS-related causes. Yet the bed's vacancy has an element of hopefulness as well—the missing occupants might return to fill the soft indentations left by their bodies. The placement of such an intimate space in a public arena can also be read as a commentary on gay rights in the 1980s and early 1990s. An earlier Gonzalez-Torres billboard project alluded to a 1986 Supreme Court ruling that gay men and women have no right to privacy or protection from the law, even in their own homes or bedrooms.[1] Both these possible meanings may live simultaneously in the intentionally ambiguous image; the work's interpretation lies open to the public and the array of associations, memories, and feelings that they bring.

Within Gonzalez-Torres's relatively short career before his death in 1996 from AIDS, he created a significant, poetic body of work. Gonzalez-Torres is often viewed through an art historical framework; his art blends the pared-down aesthetics of Minimalist and post-Minimalist art, the intellectual underpinnings of Conceptual art, a Duchampian use of the readymade, and an interest in politics, gender, and identity found in much artwork of the 1980s. More importantly, his work reenvisions these art historical movements or styles, creating new perspectives from which to view them. Through the manipulation of a set of signature motifs—piles of candy, jigsaw puzzles, curtains, paper stacks, light bulbs, and bead curtains—Gonzalez-Torres navigated through topics from politics, AIDS, love, and loss, to artistic originality.

Gonzalez-Torres's exploration of the meaning of "public" art, as seen in his billboard project, continues in his paper stacks and candy spills. His paper stacks consist of piles of offset printed paper placed directly on the gallery or museum floor; the candy spills are made of hundreds or thousands of pounds of wrapped candy laid on the floor like a rug or poured in a corner of the gallery. Gonzalez-Torres invites viewers to take a piece of paper or candy; the work gradually disappears, but ultimately can be replenished and the process begun again. Although the numerous stacks and spills he created throughout his career vary in appearance and intent, the project as a whole subverts the museum's desire to preserve and present an original, "one-of-a kind" object, which is not to be touched by viewers. Although a museum may own one of these works, in

*left page:*
Felix Gonzalez-Torres,
*Untitled,*
1991,
New York City

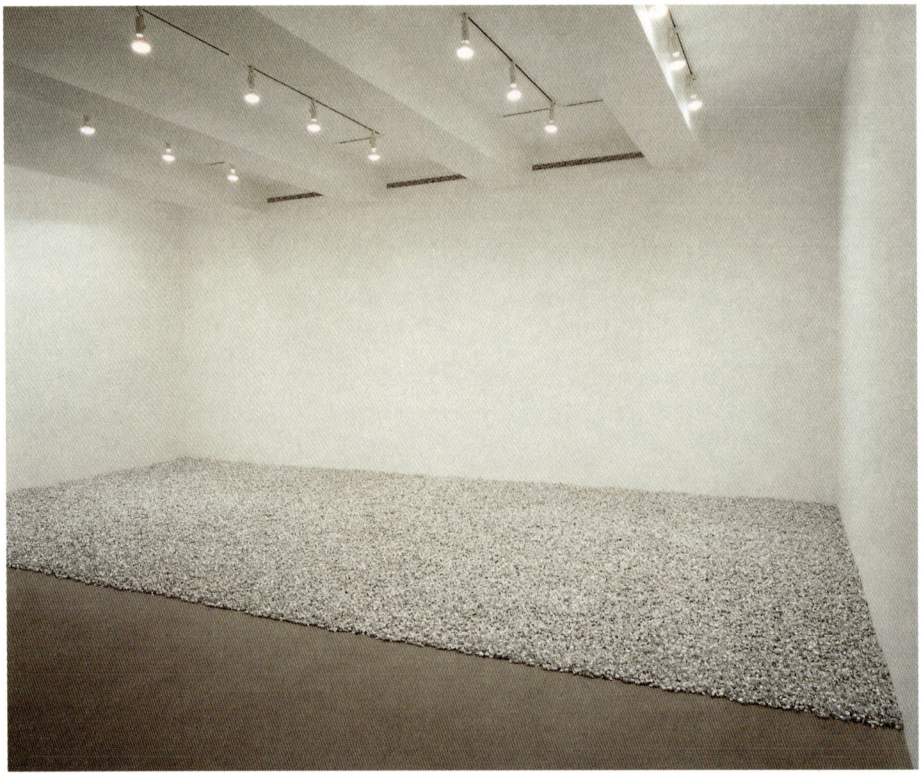

Felix Gonzalez-Torres, *Untitled (Placebo)*, 1991, Installation at Museum of Modern Art, New York

essence the art is constantly dispersed, as visitors take home (or eat!) their own "Felix Gonzalez-Torres" work of art.

Along with the philosophical or art historical implications of the stacks and spills in general, each individual work tells a specific story. In 1990, Gonzalez-Torres made a paper stack called *Untitled (Death by Gun)*; on each piece of paper is a black and white reproduction of a page from *Time* magazine carrying the names and faces of the 464 people killed by guns in one week in the United States.[2] Gonzalez-Torres takes this serial, repetitive image and further intensifies its impact by replicating it endlessly. The infinite supply of paper may represent the trivial, "throw-away" manner in which life is often regarded; both paper and life are easily taken, although ultimately renewed. Yet Gonzalez-Torres's deadpan, dispassionate presentation of a decidedly loaded image recalls Andy Warhol's silkscreens of car crashes and electric chairs—does the image become more or less powerful through repetition?

The artist's 1991 *Untitled (Placebo)* is similarly confrontational. Yet, as with all of Gonzalez-Torres's work, the presentation is subtle and ultimately ambiguous. Consisting of 1000 pounds of silver-wrapped candies, the work could refer to the AIDS epidemic and the clinical drug trials in which many AIDS patients participate, knowing that they may receive a drug that could cure them or a placebo. However, as Simon Watney states in "In Purgatory: The Work of Felix Gonzalez-Torres": "a placebo is never an inert substance, for it inevitably carries with it a profound supplement of hope."[3] Much like a placebo, all of Gonzalez-Torres's candy spills and paper stacks contain a message of hope. The gradual "death" of his stacks and spills through the viewers' consumption only leads to the rebirth and resurrection of the piece as whole again.

EM

1 Nancy Spector, *Felix Gonzalez-Torres* (Santiago de Compostela: Centro Galego de Arte Contemporánea, 1995), p. 23.
2 Ibid., p. 50.
3 Simon Watney, "In Purgatory: The Work of Felix Gonzalez-Torres" in *Parkett*, no. 39 (Zurich, 1994), p. 42.

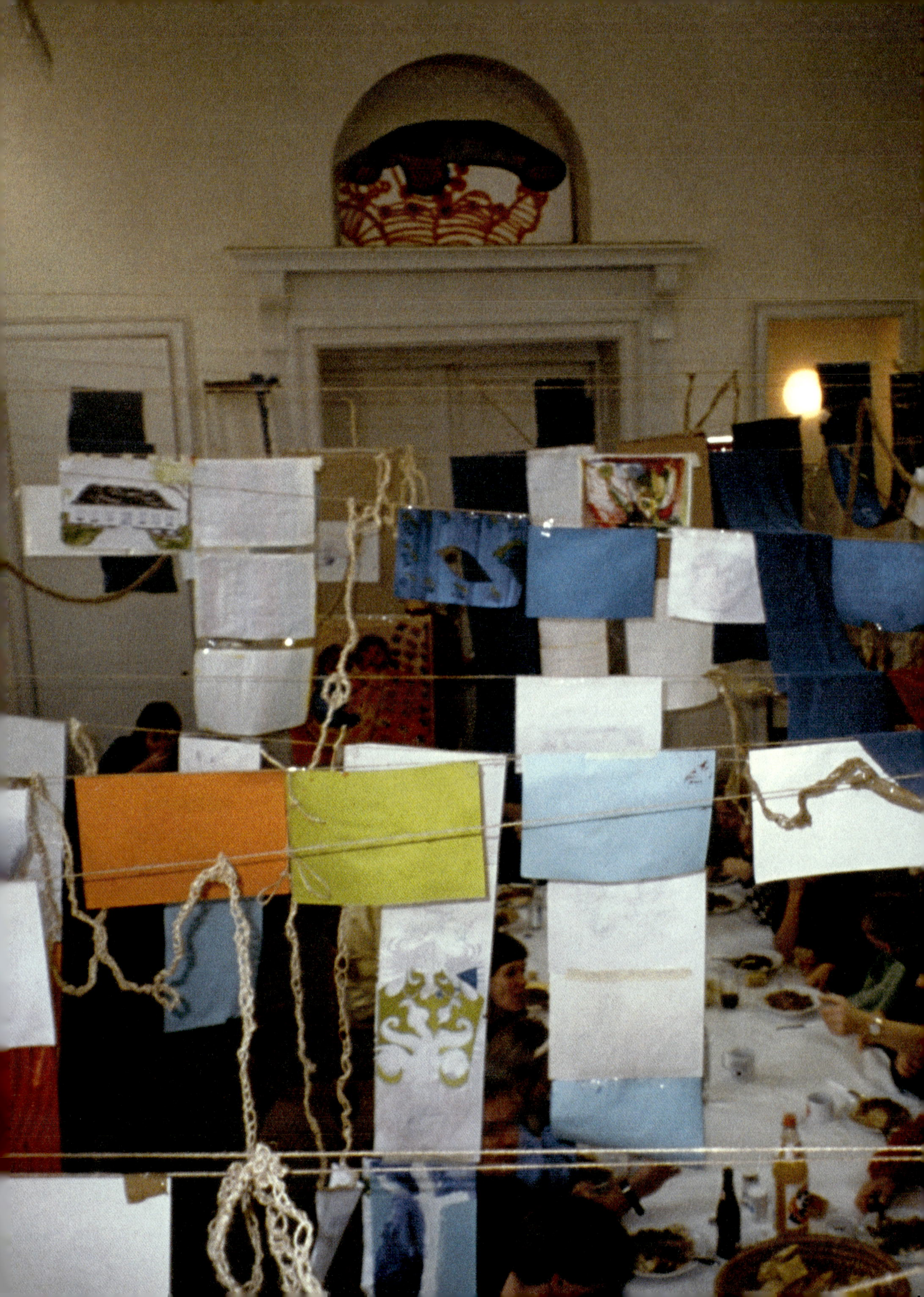

## IRENE AND CHRISTINE HOHENBÜCHLER

Born in Vienna, Austria, 1964. Live in Berlin (Christine) and Vienna (Irene).

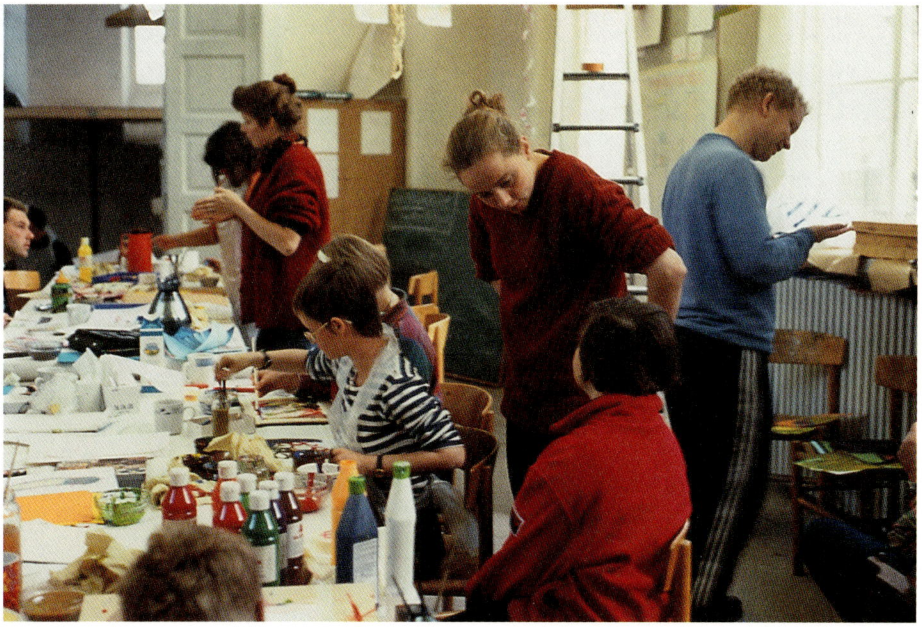

Irene and Christine Hohenbüchler, Project with students in Copenhagen, 1998

We have been trained to understand that art is not necessarily a beautiful object or indeed an object at all. Readymades, installations, performances, conceptual art—all of these things have considerably expanded our concept of art. But Irene and Christine Hohenbüchler attack a notion that has seldom been questioned: that of the author, a sure value that many people believed they could count on in the final analysis (and if possible that author was supposed to be an inspired genius, because romantic myths have proved to be long-lived). These two Austrian artists, twin sisters, have stood the idea of art as individual expression on its head and reformulated the notion of the author. They did this first by renouncing their egos in order to create with "four hands." Then, in what they call *Multiple Autorenschaft/Multiple Authorship*, they collaborate with groups of people generally drawn from institutions outside the world of art: the handicapped, the mentally retarded, prisoners, children, people with learning disabilities, and so on. These collaborations last anywhere from weeks to years (their collaboration with the Kustwerkstatt of Lienz, an institution for handicapped adults, dates back to 1990 and has given rise to a series of works exhibited under the generic title *Herbar*), during which the sisters join with others to conceive projects in which they work not only as co-artists but also as mediators, interpreters of the creativity and energy of the other participants.

Depending on the group involved and the project, the results of these efforts have varied widely, drawing on elements of all sorts of artistic practices (painting, sculpture, drawing, design, video) as well as activities traditionally associat-

*left page:*
Irene and Christine Hohenbüchler, Project with students in Copenhagen, 1998

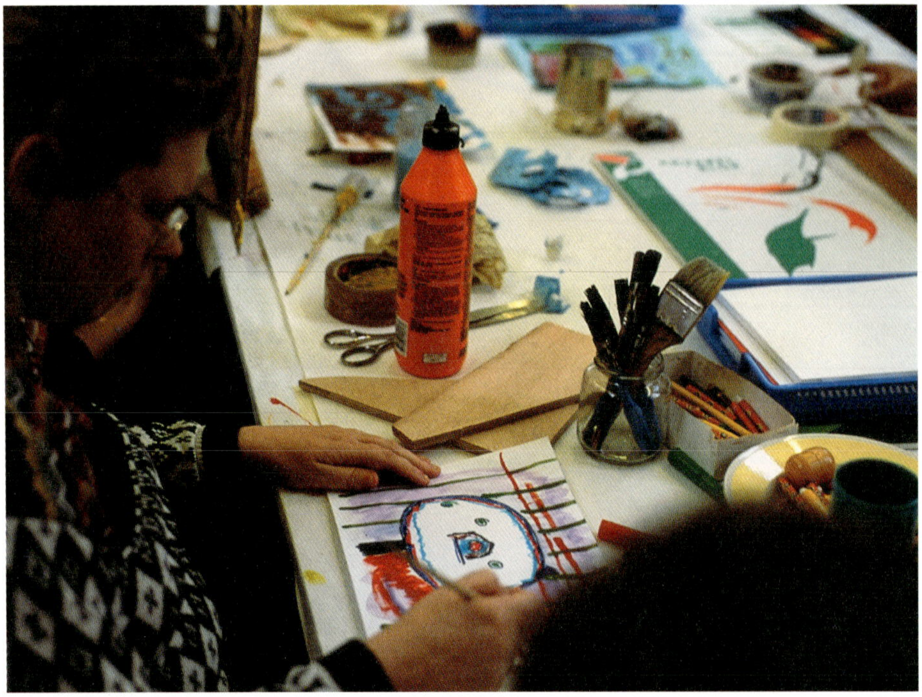

Irene and Christine Hohenbüchler, Project with students in Copenhagen, 1998

ed with the applied arts and even "manual labor" (pottery, embroidery, weaving, knitting, and various kinds of "bricolage," or tinkering). The outcome is never determined in advance, but whatever these efforts produce is always shown in a public exhibition. This is perhaps the most transgressive aspect of their work. By integrating this "marginal" art into the institutional framework of contemporary art, they initiate communication between two alien entities and create a new dynamic, which bestows value on those whose creations are granted artistic status while questioning the narrow—institutional—vision of art held by others.

In this respect their work echoes the thinking of Beuys, whose declaration that "every man is an artist" called upon us to expand our concept of art and creativity, asking us both to look for the source of creativity that exists in each individual and to extricate art from the exclusive circles of a hegemonic culture. One sees a variant of Beuys's concept of "expanded art" in the installations of Christine and Irene Hohenbüchler/Multiple Authorship. At Documenta X in 1997 and on numerous other occasions (Camden Art Center, London 2000), they created "global" works proposing several levels of imbricated meaning functioning as "rhizomes" (a term they like to use): manufactured objects are inserted in a mise-en-scène (the elegant *Kommunikationsmöbel*, networks of hemp, cork boards, etc.), which often includes a description of its own "process" (video, slides, files, narratives). The installation functions throughout the show as both a work of art and a space of exchange and communication. It also represents, in its entirety (that is, both in its material aspects and in the situations it generates), a "passage" between two realities.

Pursuing this logic of conquering other "territories" for art, Christine and Irene Hohenbüchler presented the *Mutter-Kind(er)-Haus/Mother-Child(ren) House* in the Austrian Pavilion of the Venice Biennale of 1999. This was the prototype of a prefabricated modular house (produced in collaboration with the architect Martin Feiersinger) designed as a home for women and children who were refugees from the war in Kosovo, and its clearly utilitarian function gave rise to numerous discussions, as if such a pragmatic approach (creating a work of art as a solution for a social problem) were taboo in this artistic context.

This determination to reorient artistic practice in light of social concerns is not the only direction their work has taken. Along with the works of "Multiple Authorship," the Hohenbüchlers have continued to work as a duo (curtain for the Vienna Opera House, 1999), further complicating the task of anyone who would confine them to a single category.

Not simply artists and not merely social activists, they escape and undermine all invariably reductive binary categorizations (high art/popular art, artist/non-artist, work of art/functional object) and make sport of boundaries that they cannot abolish. Their work thus brings out the ambiguity and ambivalence in the world of contemporary art, a vital and joyous confusion that calls to mind the formula of Robert Filliou: "Art is that which makes life more interesting than art."

SM

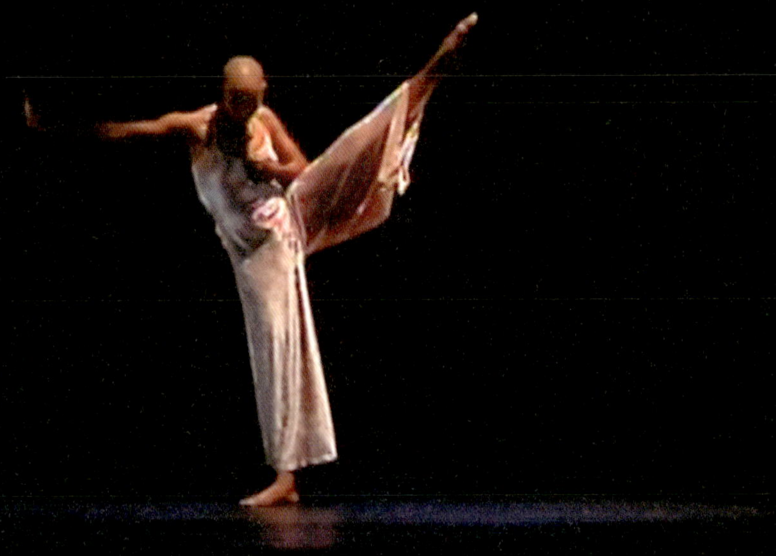

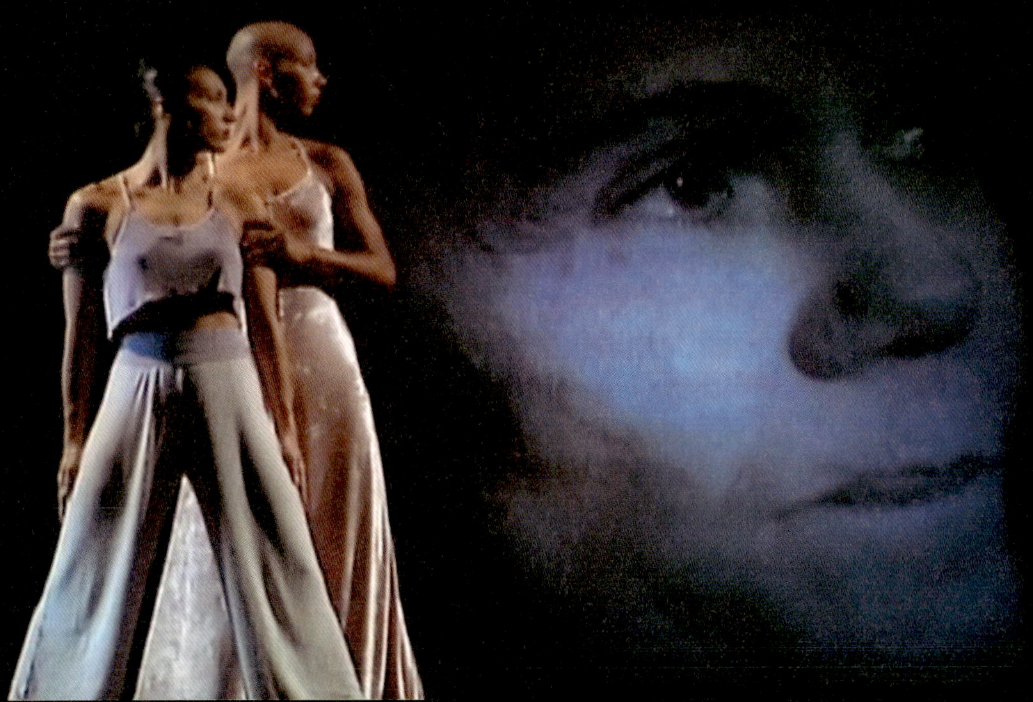

**BILL T. JONES**

Born in Bunnell, Florida, 1952. Lives in New York City.

**GRETCHEN BENDER**

Born in Seaford, Delaware, 1951. Lives in New York City.

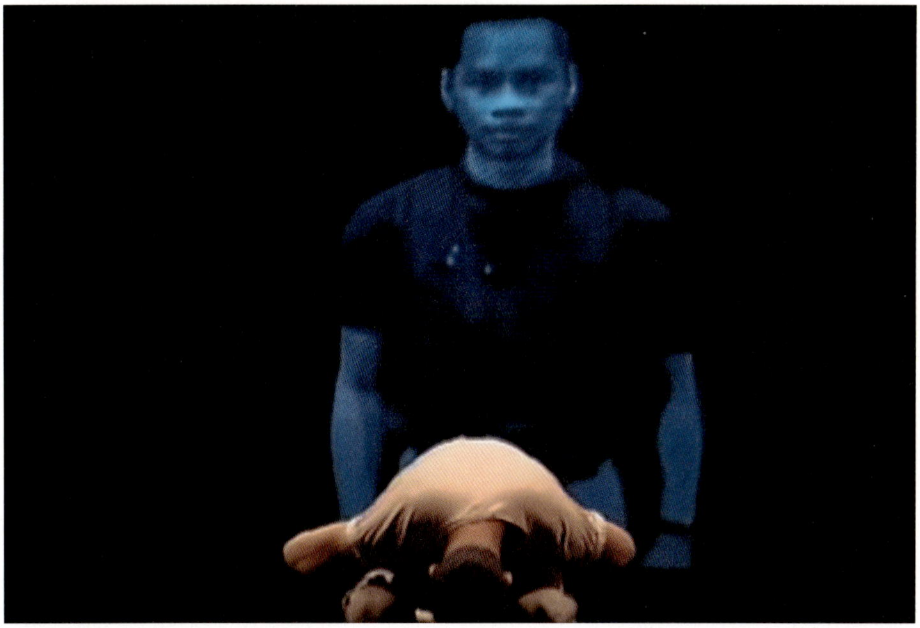

Bill T. Jones and Gretchen Bender, still from video of *Still/Here*, 1994

*Still/Here*, a provocative multimedia dance event by dancer and choreographer Bill T. Jones, premiered in 1994 in Lyons, France and was greeted by an effusive standing ovation at the finale. A moving fusion of dance, music, song, and video, *Still/Here* is Jones's meditation on life, illness, and mortality. Other works throughout Jones's career have touched upon these topics; after the death of his long-time dance partner and companion, Arnie Zane, from AIDS-related causes, Jones made *Forsythia* (1989), a duet that reflected on Zane's passing, but also on Jones's attempts to heal and move forward. But with *Still/Here*, Jones, who is HIV-positive, wanted to create a dance that would not just be a personal expression of his struggle to live while facing a life-threatening illness, but a more universal representation of what this type of experience means: "I would shape a work that transcended difference. I would…shape it around the ideal of commonality."[1]

For inspiration, Jones looked to other people who had met similar challenges. He organized fourteen Survival Workshops in eleven cities; the participants were "of all ages, classes, races, sexual preferences, and states of health."[2] Ranging from age 11 to 74, they shared the fact that they each grappled with a serious illness. In the workshops, participants made drawings, gestural and video portraits of themselves, and answered challenging, intimate questions about their illness: *How did you feel at the moment of diagnosis? Take us to your death. How do you*

*left page:*
Bill T. Jones and Gretchen Bender, still from video of *Still/Here*, 1994

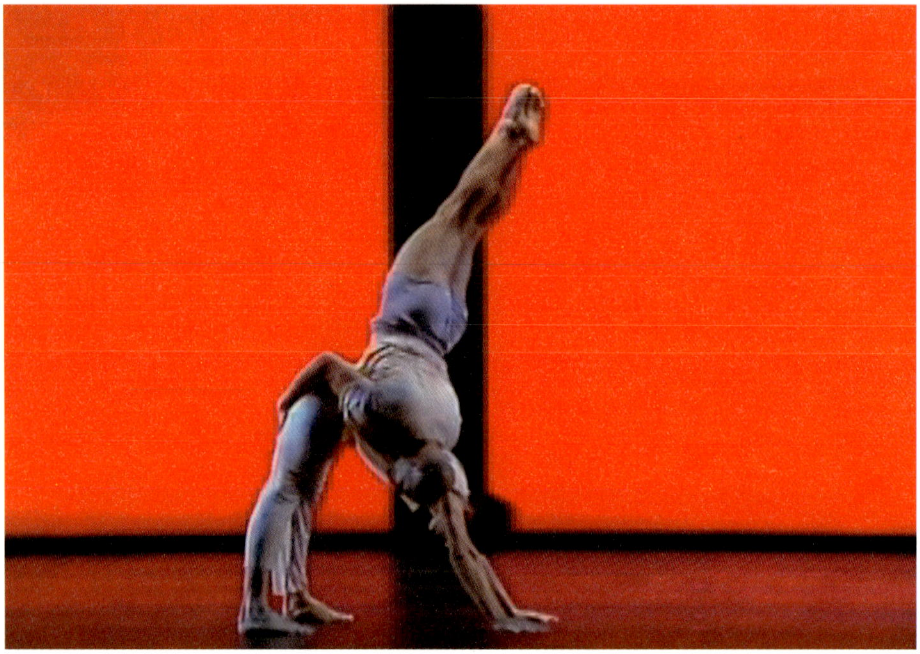

Bill T. Jones and Gretchen Bender, still from video of *Still/Here*, 1994

*look? Who's there with you?* Gretchen Bender, a media artist who has collaborated with the Bill T. Jones/Arnie Zane Dance Company since the 1980s, videotaped all of the sessions; early on in *Still/Here*'s development, Jones decided that Bender's video work would be a key component of the final piece. The workshops, and their documentation, provided Jones and Bender with the material that would inspire the movements and imagery of *Still/Here.*

As the title of the work suggests, *Still/Here* consists of two parts, each with a distinct choreography, sound, and mood. The composers, singers, and musicians that contributed to *Still/Here* were central to the creation of an individual voice for each section. During Jones's career he has frequently collaborated with some of the most influential and inventive artists, musicians, and thinkers of the moment. In 1985, the artist Keith Haring designed the sets for Jones's and Zane's *Secret Pastures*; Jones incorporated artist Jenny Holzer's textual *Truisms* into a duet with Lawrence Goldhuber in *Holzer Duets...Truisms* (1985); for *Degga* (1995), Jones collaborated with author Toni Morrison and jazz percussionist Max Roach.

*Still/Here*'s collaborators are similarly dynamic. In the first section, *Still*, composer Kenneth Frazelle's classically styled, solemn music is sung by folksinger Odetta and played by the Lark String Quartet. The dancers assume characters from the workshops, not impersonating them, but through action interpreting some of the feelings and ideas expressed in the workshops. Large video monitors, projecting imagery culled from the Survival Workshop footage, as well as abstracted, constructed images inspired by participants' testimony, move in and out of the space, sometimes carried by dancers. For *Still/Here*'s second part,

*Here*, Vernon Reid, guitarist from the rock band Living Color, composed the music—weaving fragments of sounds from workshop recordings with "moody, pop, jazz, blues riffs."[3] The colors on the stage become more vibrant—the dancers wear blood red, rust, and orange-colored costumes and the lighting moves to sometimes disco-like oranges and yellows. Conceptually, between the first and second section, the work shifts from exploring the individual, interior experience of confronting a life-threatening illness to reflecting on how one interacts with a larger community and society at such a time. *Still/Here*, as the title implies, is not a dance about death, but rather an emphatic statement about the possibilities of the living.

EM

1 Bill T. Jones, with Peggy Gillespie, *Last Night on Earth* (New York: Pantheon Books, 1995), p. 251.
2 Ibid., p. 252.
3 Ibid., p. 256.

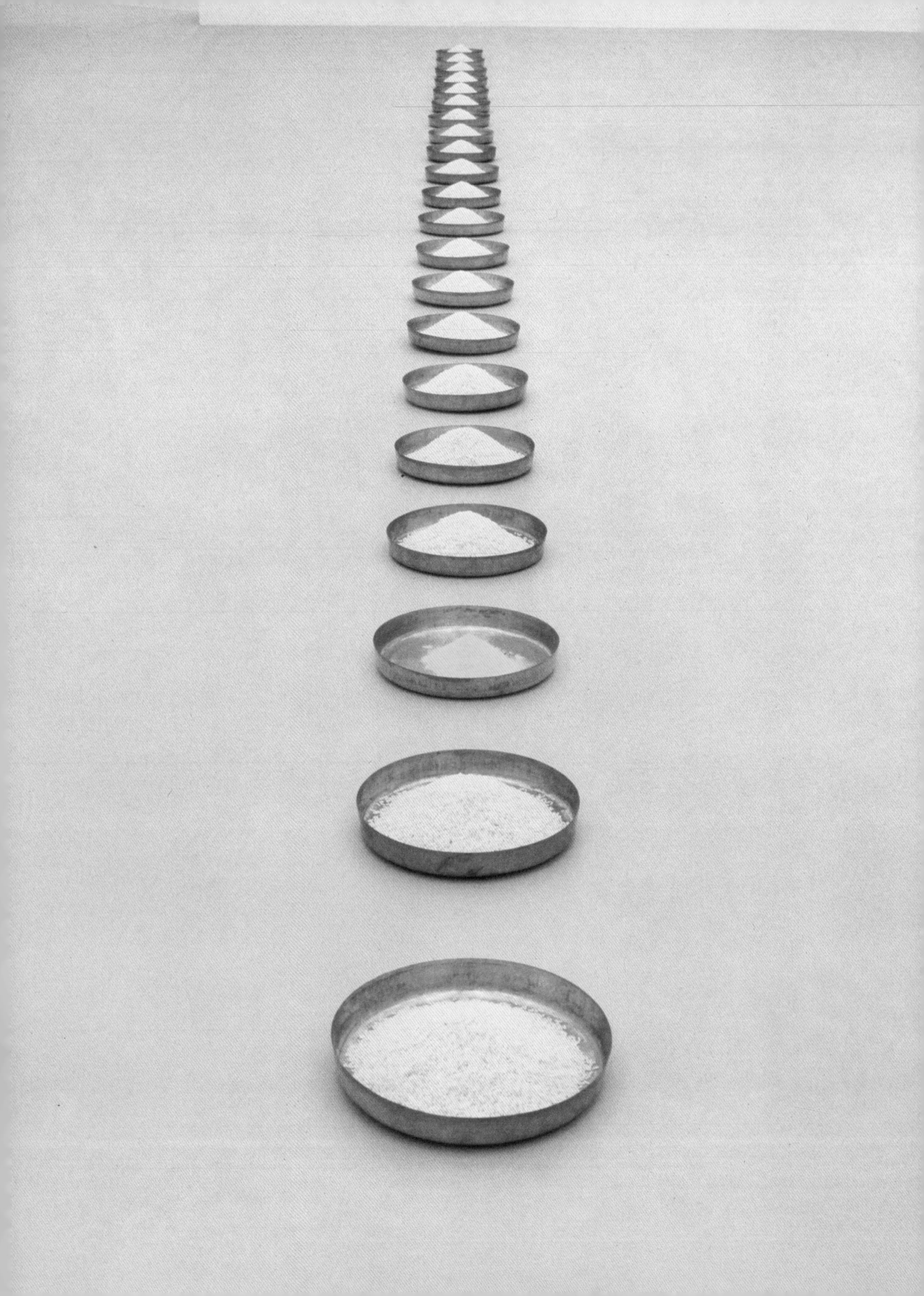

## WOLFGANG LAIB

Born in Metzingen, Germany, 1950. Lives in Hochdorf near Biberach, Germany.

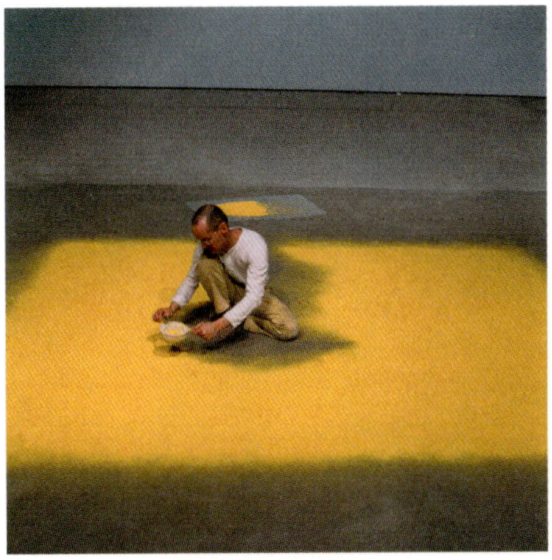

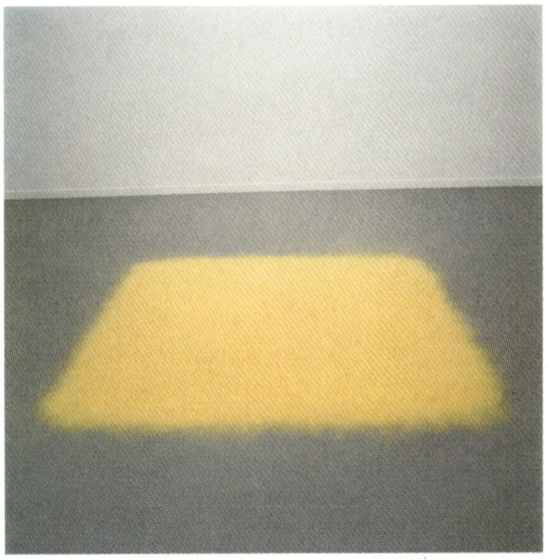

*left:*
Wolfgang Laib,
*Pollen from Hazelnut,*
1992

*right:*
Wolfgang Laib,
*Pollen from Pine,*
1999

Wolfgang Laib became a doctor in 1974, but has never practiced medicine. Upon finishing medical school, Laib decided to become an artist, due to what he described as "a deep tension and fundamental unhappiness about examining the human body and ignoring the soul."[1] While medicine aims to bring about tangible transformations of the body, Laib, through his quiet, contemplative works, hopes to create spiritual, rather than corporal, change. Laib has slowly built up a repertoire of carefully chosen materials—milk, pollen, rice, and beeswax—which are linked by their natural and life-giving qualities. Forming these evocative materials into basic, almost primal shapes such as cones, squares, houses, and ziggurats, Laib creates artworks that act as religion-less icons or universal meditations on life, ritual, and beauty.

In 1975, Laib made his first milkstone, a sculptural form that he continues to produce today. The milkstones consist of a square piece of marble placed directly on the floor. Laib carves a slight indentation along the top of the polished surface, which is then filled with milk; the liquid, virtually the same color as the marble, floats on top of the stone, replacing the missing marble. The milkstones can be seen as a reinterpretation of the hard-edged minimalist sculpture of Donald Judd, Carl Andre, and Tony Smith. Laib softens the stability and geometry of the marble slab by juxtaposing it with the milk's fluidity and sinuous edges. While 1960s and 1970s minimalism was often made from mass-produced materials through processes which the artist was not involved in, Laib's milkstones are not only hand-carved and polished, but require the daily ritual of pouring fresh milk onto the work.

Outside of this Western art historical context, the milkstones additionally reference Laib's interest in Eastern philosophy and religion. In Buddhist and Hindu rituals, milk is often used to wash cult figures and is regularly presented as an

*left page:*
Wolfgang Laib,
*The Rice Meals,*
1983

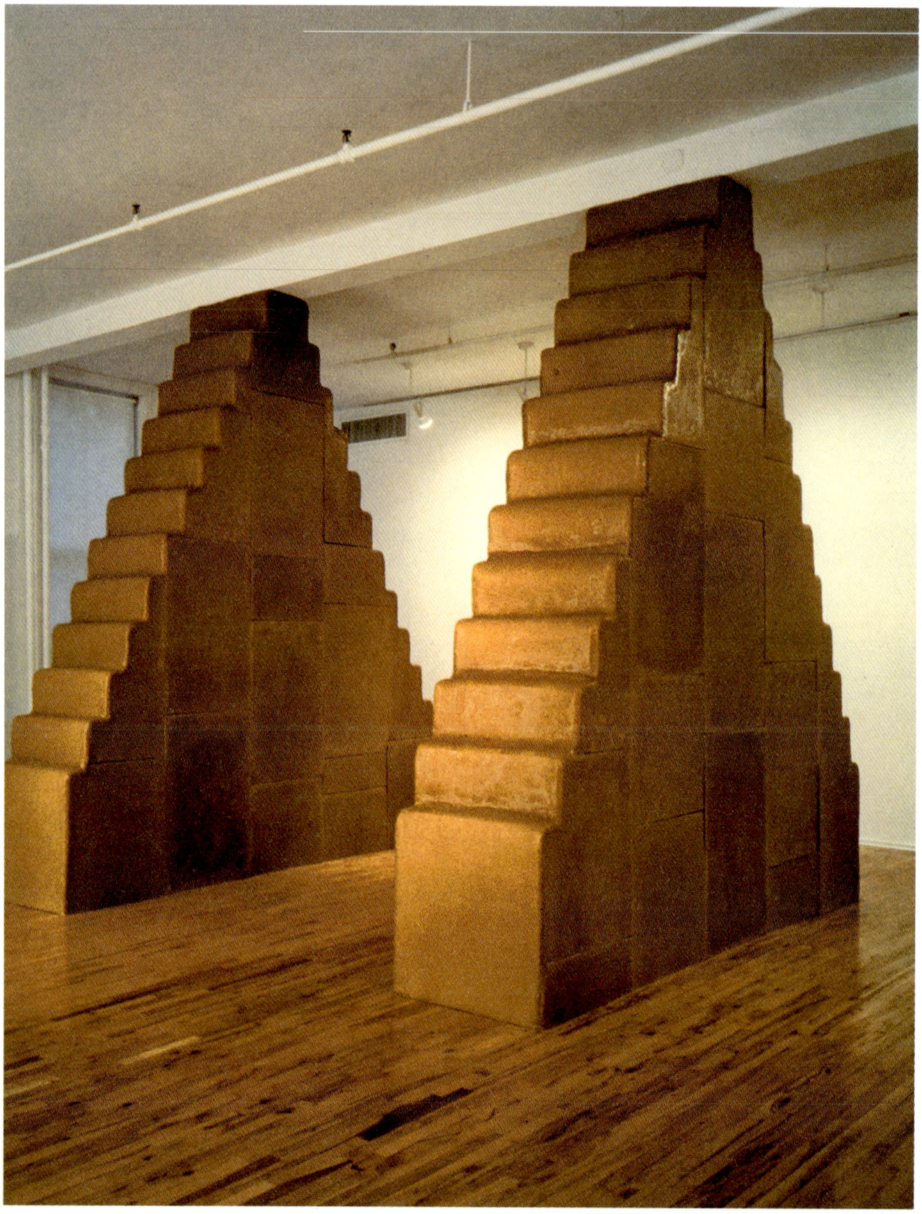

Wolfgang Laib,
*Nowhere-Everywhere*,
1998

offering to gods. In his youth, Laib's family traveled extensively throughout Asia and the Middle East, visiting Turkey, Iran, Afghanistan, and India. This influence is also present in Laib's work with rice. *The Rice Meals* (1983) consists of 33 brass plates placed in a line; each is filled with a pile of rice, except for one that holds hazelnut pollen. In India, these plates are used for eating meals, as well as containers for temple offerings of food or flowers. In this context, rice, like milk, blends the quotidian and the sacred. It is mundane and abundant, yet essential for life and spiritually symbolic.

Since 1977, Laib has been collecting pollen from the trees and plants near his home in southern Germany. After gathering different types of pollen—birch, elm, hazelnut, pine, moss, and dandelion—into jars, Laib composes with these fine, fragile powders. He heaps the pollen into tiny mountains as in *The Rice Meals* or sifts it directly onto the gallery or museum floor, creating monochromatic squares of pure color that seem to hover above the ground. The life-giving potential of such a large amount of pollen is great, yet the works are equally delicate and could be easily destroyed. While the pollen squares—glowing, wispy patches of color—have been likened to abstract paintings by Mark Rothko and Yves Klein, Laib's pollen squares *are* color, rather than representations of color. They are akin to natural readymades; Laib presents pollen rather than making something with it. When viewed in the starkness of a white gallery they are reminders of their remote origin and of Laib's time-consuming, laborious process in realizing them. His meditative, patient work in the fields of rural Germany provides a stark contrast to the often-quick pace of contemporary life. At the same time, within the exhibition context, the pollen becomes entirely alien from its source and appears artificial, as well as organic. With its pollinating potential denied, it becomes an object of contemplation rather than possibility.

Laib presents common, overlooked materials in radically simple ways and in doing so makes visible their complexity. The processes involved in the creation of his work—the replenishment of the milkstones, the seasonal gathering of pollen—suggest the cyclical nature of life and the rituals that give meaning to it.

EM

1 David Galloway, "Pollen Alert," in *ArtNews* 99 (October 2000), p. 168.

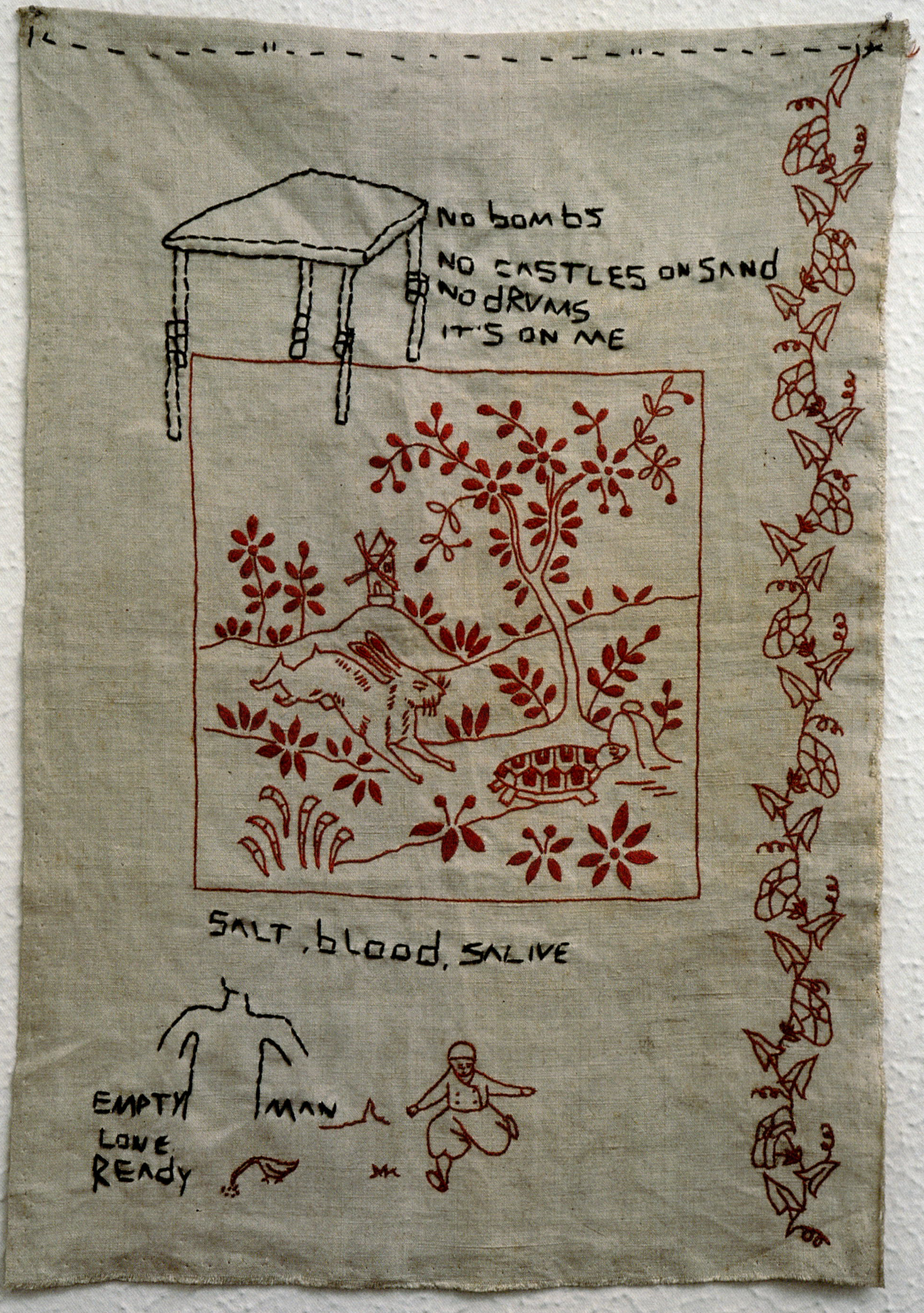
No bombs
NO CASTLES ON SAND
NO dRUMS
IT'S ON ME
SALT, blood, SALIVE
EMPTY
MAN
LOVE
ReAdy

## LEONILSON

Born in Fortaleza, Caera, Brazil, 1957. Died in São Paulo, Brazil, 1993.

Relatively unknown outside his native Brazil, Leonilson's work blends the native influence of northeastern Brazilian arts and crafts and religious iconography with the symbolically charged image making of the 1980s *Transavanguardia* painters. His paintings from the 1980s and 90s are typically thinly painted acrylics on raw unstretched canvas. The imagery suggests a personal iconography of repeated forms, including an angel-like figure that is ambiguously male; a volcano form; and jewels. The limited vocabulary is used sparingly, but despite its apparent simplicity the varying combinations of characters adds up to a

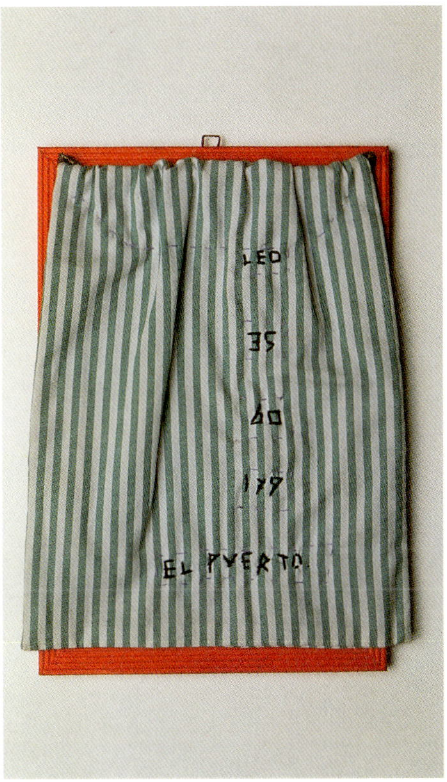


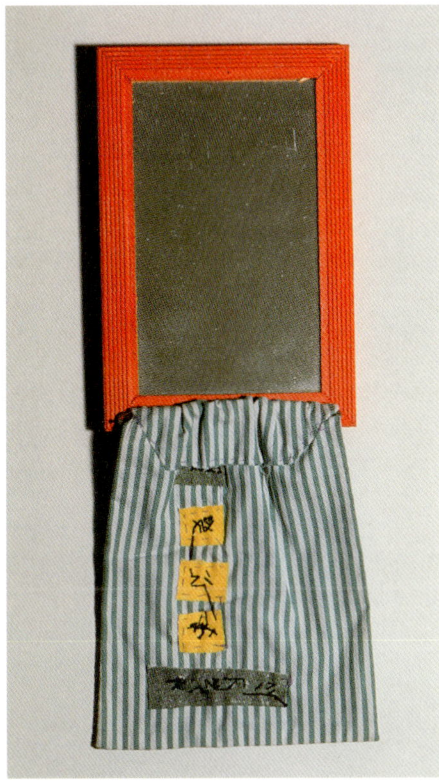

Leonilson, *El Puerto,* 1992. Collection of Famíla Bezerra Dias, São Paulo

complex and metaphorically powerful language. The illustrative style borrows not only from artists such as Francesco Clemente but also the graffiti imagery of Keith Haring and post-Pop art. However, Leonilson has none of Clemente's mysticism—his imagery remains resistant to such outright romanticism—and shows little interest in commercial culture, either as a critique or a reflection of changing times.

Many of Leonilson's symbolic forms appear to have fluctuated initially between three and two dimensions. After traveling extensively in Europe in the 1980s and witnessing the work of Joseph Beuys, Arte Povera, and the New

*left page:* Leonilson, *Empty Man,* 1991. Collection of Famíla Bezerra Dias, São Paulo

British Sculptors such as Richard Long, Leonilson exhibited sculptural work both there and in Brazil. Consisting of sparely constructed forms in the shape of interconnected and enigmatic towers (or volcanoes), spirals, spheres, and crosses, Leonilson's installations suggest the type of communication between forms that appeared similarly in his paintings. Together the objects take on increased significance, suggesting a Beuys-like orchestration of meaning.

Increasingly in paintings and watercolors from the late 80s, Leonilson's work appears concerned with a personal narrative. Images suggestive of the artist's conflicting relationship to his Catholic upbringing and his gay sexuality begin to appear alongside a mapping or cartography of the body that is at once erotic and melancholic. Roads, arteries, or tunnel-like images begin to appear alongside the occasional use of language or words that match the imagery in their poetic intensity. The failure of language to fully express emotion or experience is hinted at, and the combination of sign and character begins to take on a heightened resonance.

In the late 1980s Leonilson began to exhibit embroidered works that reflect the influence of the untrained Brazilian artist Arthur Bispo do Rosário, whose work had come to prominence at that time. Bispo's embroidered "paintings" are elaborate narratives that contain complex iconographies; Leonilson, though clearly influenced by Bispo's media, retains his own concise use of imagery in sewn works that are minimally austere in comparison. Bispo was not the only influence for this change in media. Lygia Clark and Hélio Oiticica had both used fabric and embroidery in their work: Clark had made a variety of sewn object/outfits; and Oiticica's *Parangoles* were capes or costumes made for samba dance groups. Leonilson was also exposed to the work of the Shakers during a trip to America, and it is possible that the symbolic and mystical forms used both in drawing and embroidery by these generally self-trained artists and craftspeople affected his illustrative style.

In 1991 Leonilson tested positive for HIV. He had already been suffering from drastically ill health, and the change in his physical well-being is reflected in the subsequent development of his work. Leonilson's use of embroidery gradually became a necessity as his ability to draw and paint declined, and his imagery and language focus increasingly on tracking his state of mind and health. The works in the last years of his life, from 1991-93, can be read as self-portraits. The coupling of words and images resists the literalism of representation, but the evocative image of a rapidly deteriorating body is amply demonstrated in his choice of metaphor. *J.L.B.D.*, a simple square of orange velvet, is marked in the upper left corner with the artist's initials. The tactility of the fabric, which forms a small pocket, suggests the vulnerability of touch, and the presence of the artist's name makes the object akin to a reliquary to the self. *Empty Man*, a work that in its decorativeness more closely resembles the work of Bispo, names

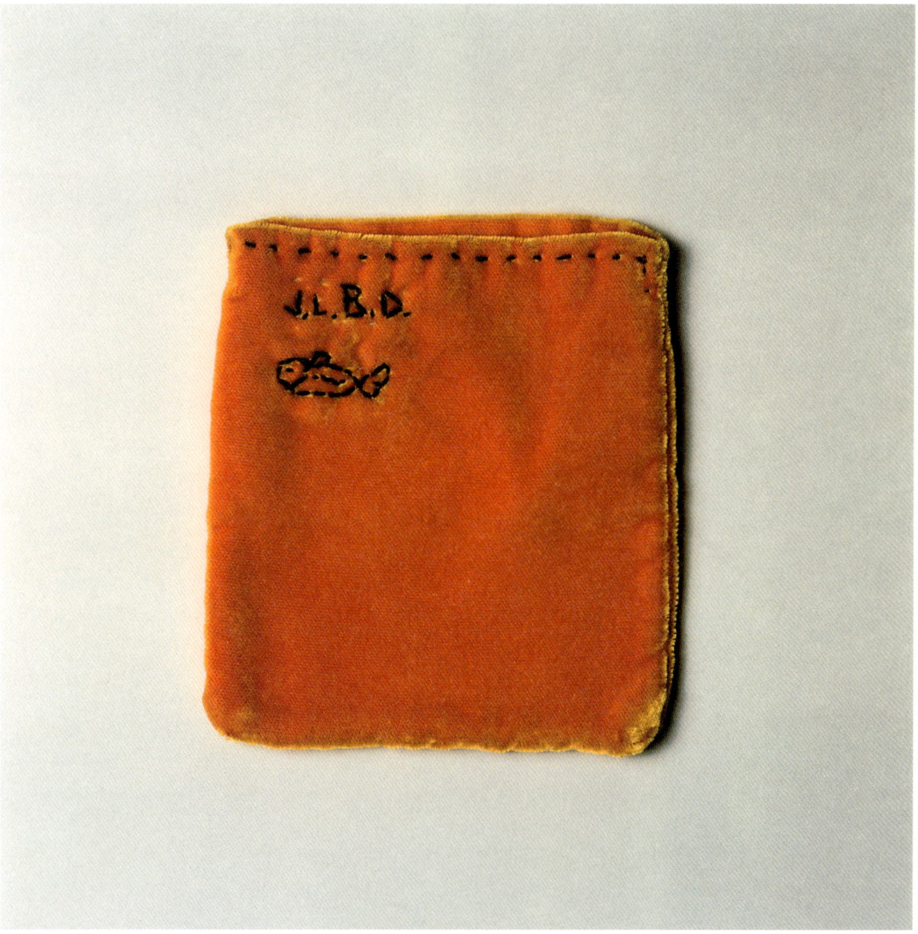


Leonilson, *J.L.B.D.*, 1992.
Collection of Famíla Bezerra Dias, São Paulo

some of the conductive substances of the body, "salt," "blood," "saliva," next to a simple torso labeled "empty man." The essence of the human body is made painfully banal, and it appears that the more familiar the artist becomes with his illness the more abstract his body appears in the work, as if this process of learning renders the opposite effect of an unknowing or separation.

*El Puerto*, one of Leonilson's most affecting late works, consists of a simple piece of mirror attached to which hangs a piece of striped cloth. Embroidered on the front are the artist's vital statistics: "Leo" (Leonilson)," "35" (his age), "60" (his weight), "179" (his height). The covered mirror reflects perhaps the horror induced by the reflection of sickness's ravaging effect, but also the frustration of representation and a loss of any sense of "reality" as a result of the brutality of such an unjust illness.

JM

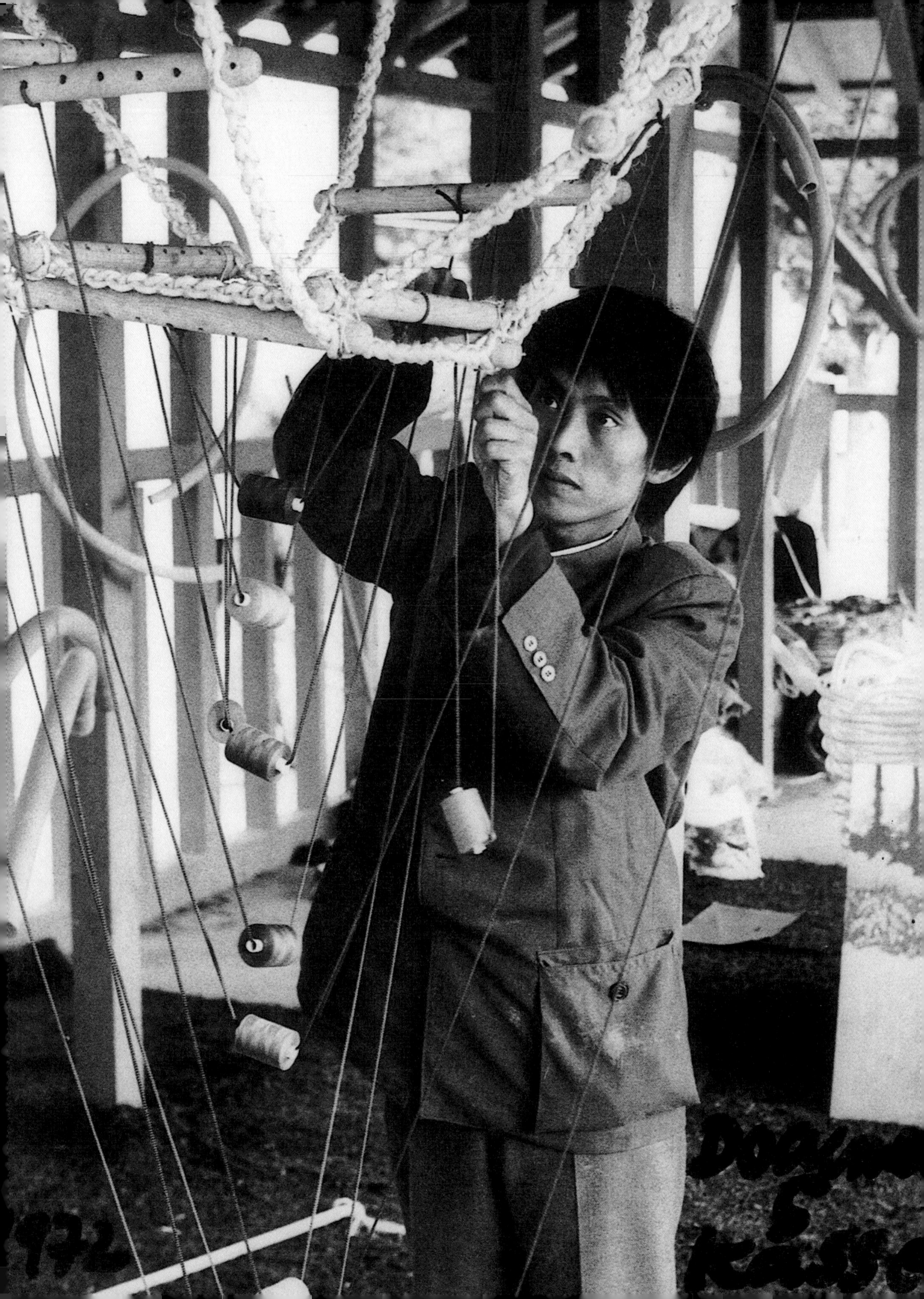
1972
5

## DAVID MEDALLA

Born in Manila, Philippines, 1942. Lives in London.

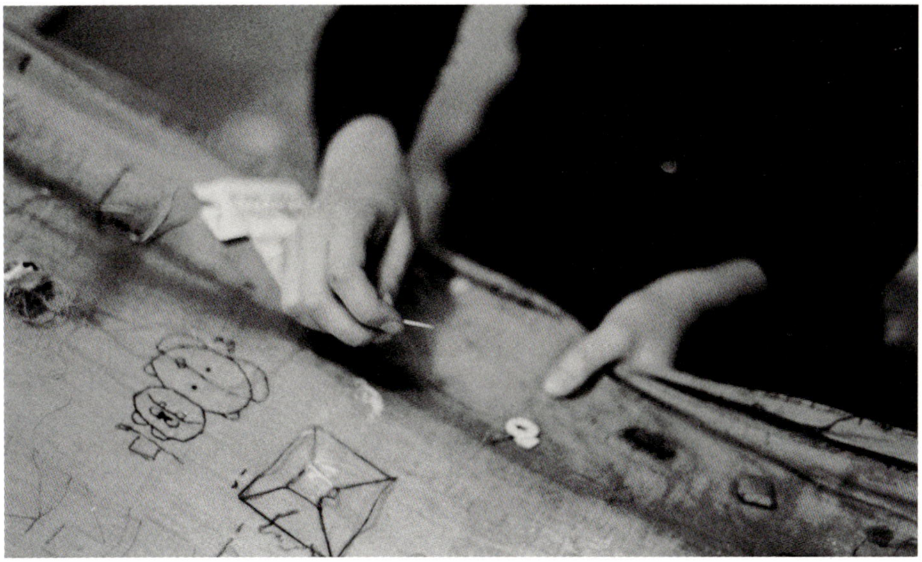

David Medalla, drawing of *A Stitch in Time*, 1967

David Medalla is virtually indefinable as an artist, perhaps because his work is so closely aligned with his life; with Medalla, it is difficult to discern where art ends and life begins. Since the 1960s, he has been traveling in every sense of the word—between countries, within cities, across art movements, and among groups of people. His artwork reflects this constant state of flux and change. Medalla's immense, multifarious oeuvre touches upon practically every genre of the late twentieth and early twenty-first century—painting, photography, sculpture, installation, and performance.

In some respects, Medalla is relatively unknown in the art world. Consciously, he has not followed the typical path for a career artist; for example, he has never been represented by a gallery or an art dealer. Yet his impact, both personally and artistically, on numerous art movements and artists has been great. Throughout his life, Medalla has been prominently involved in the creation of many influential art galleries, projects, and collaboratives, many of which aptly capture the spirit of their time. These have ranged from the Exploding Galaxy, a late 1960s performance art group, to the 1970s Artists for Democracy, an exhibition space and artists' collective that advocated for liberation movements around the world, to his current venture, the London Biennial, a free-form multi-artist event throughout the city of London. While Medalla is dedicated to the support, interpretation, and organization of artists, this work has always been essentially linked to his own art production.

In the mid-1960s, Medalla was co-director of Signals London, an art gallery known for showing kinetic art, a relatively experimental art form. Around this time, Medalla first presented his bubble machines, groupings of white boxes of

*left page:*
David Medalla,
*A Stitch in Time*,
at The Peoples' Participation Pavilion, Documenta V, Kassel, 1972

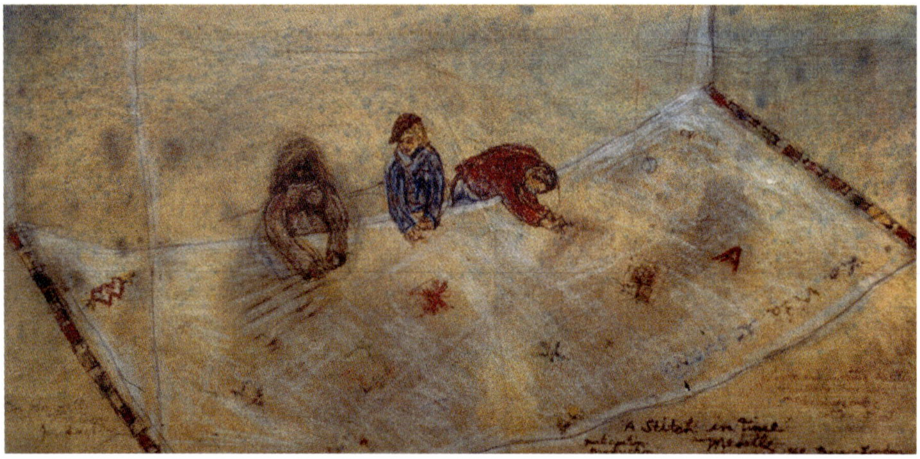

David Medalla, drawing of *A Stich in Time*, 1967

different heights and dimensions that emit clouds of bubbles. These constantly changing and shifting sculptures embody motion, rather than suggesting it statically. As sculptures, the bubble machines radically soften the natural, organic shapes found in Brancusi's work and expand upon Calder's explorations of movement and time. While the sculptures are machines, supposedly rational, controllable, and predictable things, Medalla gives his bubble machines the sculptural equivalent of free will. He removes the element of choice and the evidence of the artist's hand, allowing chance, gravity, and nature to determine the sculpture's appearance.

Medalla's interest in relinquishing artistic control is also expressed in his series of "participation-production" works produced between 1968 and 1977. These works, including *A Stitch in Time* (first presented in 1968), *Porcelain Wedding* (1973), and *Eskimo Carver* (1977), were inspired by a mixture of Buddhist texts, Marxist philosophy, and Medalla's travels to Third World countries. The "participation-production" pieces are linked by the primary importance of spectator involvement in the completion of the artwork. *A Stitch in Time* consists of suspended cotton fabric, rope, and spools of thread; viewers are encouraged to use the thread to embroider whatever they please onto the fabric. While museum and gallery-going has historically been a passive, hands-off event, *A Stitch in Time* not only allows viewers to touch, but to become instrumental in the ongoing construction of the piece. Rather than being exhibited as a finished work of art, it evolves and changes over time, with new meanings stitched into it for every person who contributes to the piece. Medalla intends the work to have a healing aspect: "stitching, like all forms of needlework, has a very therapeutic value, because you have to concentrate not only in threading the needle, but in making your statement, whatever it is."[1] *A Stitch in Time* has been exhibited numerous times since 1968, with each new venue creating its own unique version. These are not "recreations" of the original piece, but more like satellite versions of one large work that stretches across time and space.

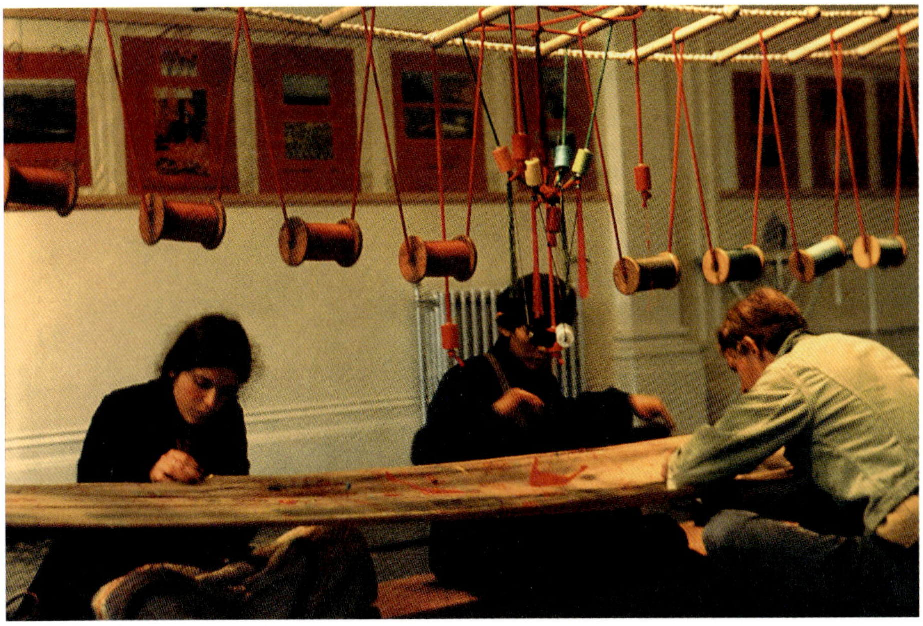

David Medalla,
*A Stitch in Time*,
installed at "A Survey of the Avant Garde in Britain, Part 1",
Gallery House, London,
1972

While any sweeping declarations regarding the trajectory of Medalla's career are bound to have exceptions, since the late 1970s his work has focused more on explorations of himself. One example of this is his ongoing series of almost twenty years, *Impromptus,* a collection of photographs and short, spontaneous performances. They embody Medalla's chameleon-like persona and his wanderings throughout his home of London and the world. *Psychic Self-Defence* (1983) pictures Medalla in front of Westminster in London; he wears a makeshift mask made from a book jacket and he holds a small bust of Mozart in one hand and Beethoven in the other. In *A Celebration of World Mythologies in Rotterdam* (1984) Medalla covers his face with a three-dimensional nativity card he found in a flea market. Both photographs, with their use of an improvised mask, reflect Medalla's self-conception of the moment, making visible his interior, possibly fleeting, thoughts and feelings. As *Impromptus* demonstrates, Medalla's everyday experiences provide fertile ground for his art, and that art allows him to define his life.

EM

1 Guy Brett, *Exploding Galaxies: The Art of David Medalla* (London: Kala Press, 1995), p. 99.

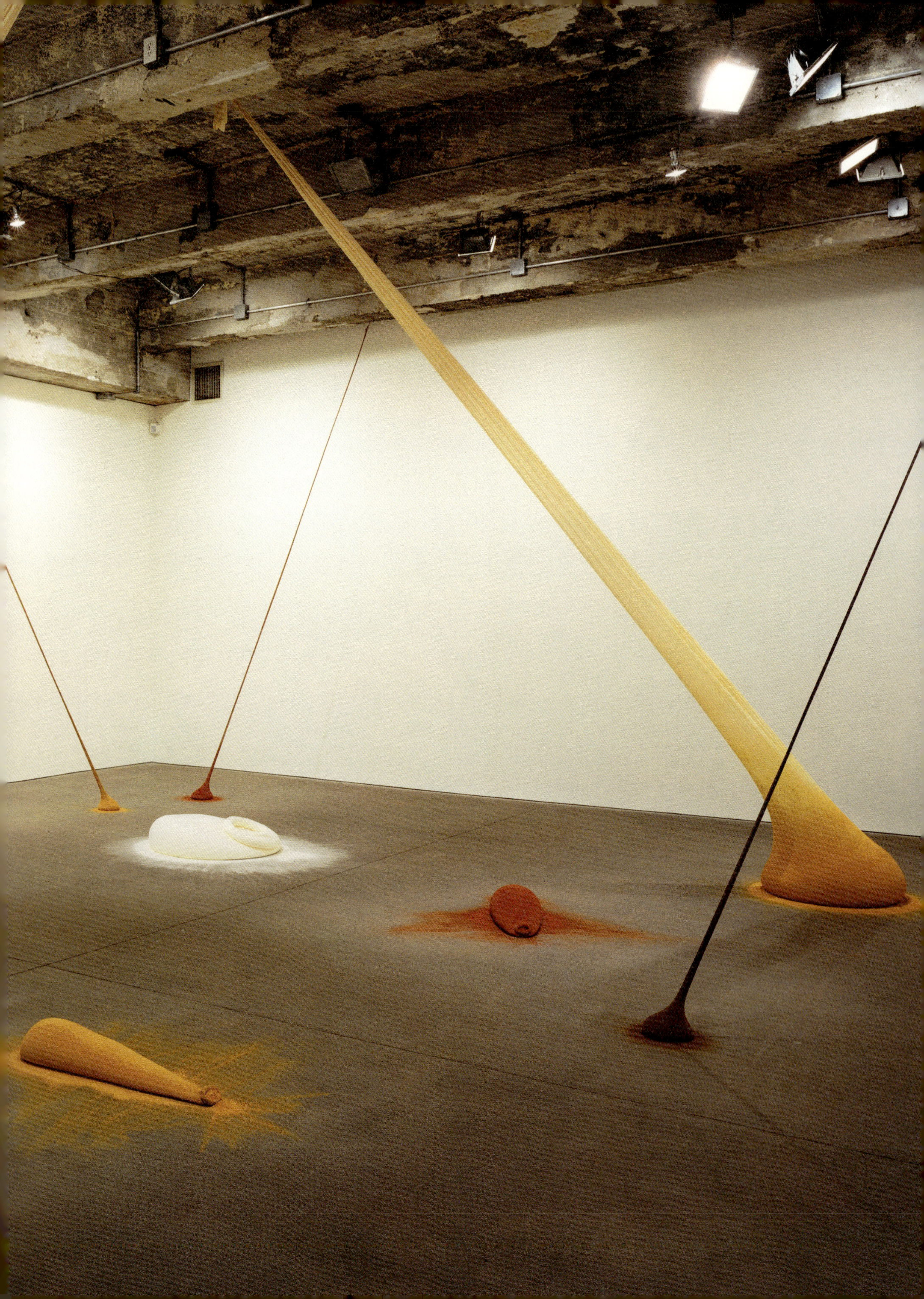

## ERNESTO NETO

Born in Rio de Janeiro, Brazil, 1964. Lives in Rio de Janeiro.

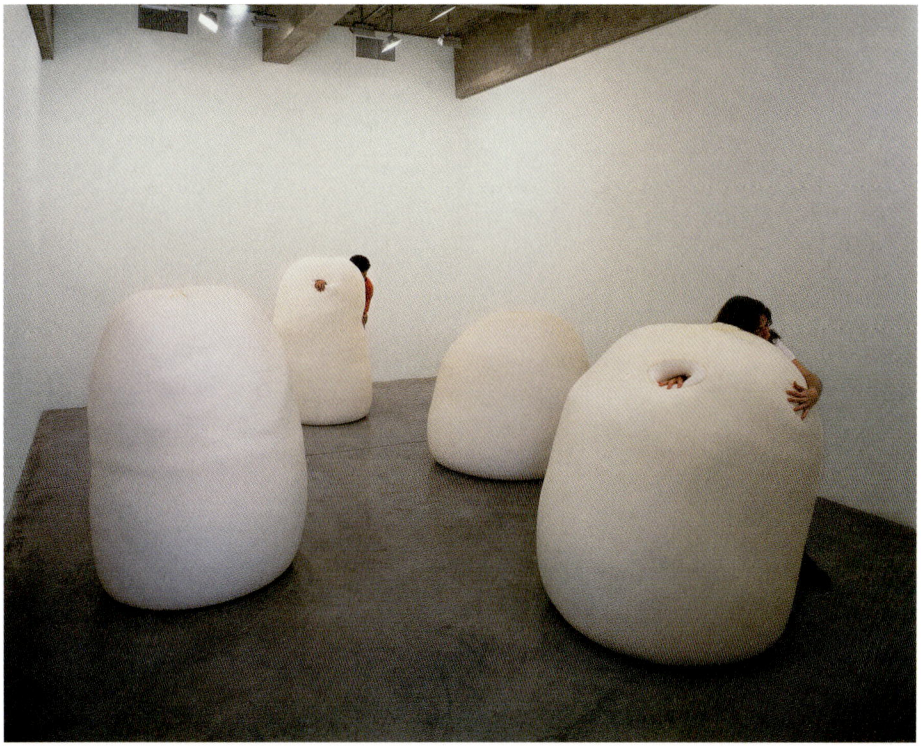

Ernesto Neto,
*The Ovaloids' Meeting*, 1998

If minimal sculpture has in the past been regarded as somewhat cool or off-putting for viewers, Ernesto Neto's sculptures counter that impression. Neto makes nonrepresentational, minimal works that viewers can hug, smell, explore, walk into, and fall asleep in. Since the late 1980s, Neto has been using Lycra, the stretchy, pliable fabric that is used to make women's stockings, as the primary medium for his sculptures—filling it with Styrofoam pellets, tiny lead balls, and pungent spices. The simple, mysterious forms that Neto employs lead to a complex system of references, ranging from the unknown, expansive terrain of outer space to the microcosmic landscape of the inner body.

Neto's installation *Piff, Paff, Puff…Puff, Poff Puff, Piff…Piff, Paff* (1997) is a grouping of sculptures filled with assorted spices and powders such as turmeric, clove, and chili powder. To compose the work, Neto dropped long, thin pieces of fabric and smaller sacks of Lycra, both weighted with spices, from the ceiling. This process of creation, which Neto uses in many of his sculptures, allows the shapes to form through chance and gravity, lending a certain immediacy and unaffectedness to them. The work's humorous title is onomatopoeic, with the words taken from the sounds the sculptures made as they were dropped into place. The impact of the fall leaves haloes of powder around each sculpture; the vibrantly colored spices seep out of the porous fabric and onto the floor, recall-

*left page:*
Ernesto Neto,
*Piff, Paff, Puff...Puff, Poff Puff, Piff...Piff, Paff*,
1997

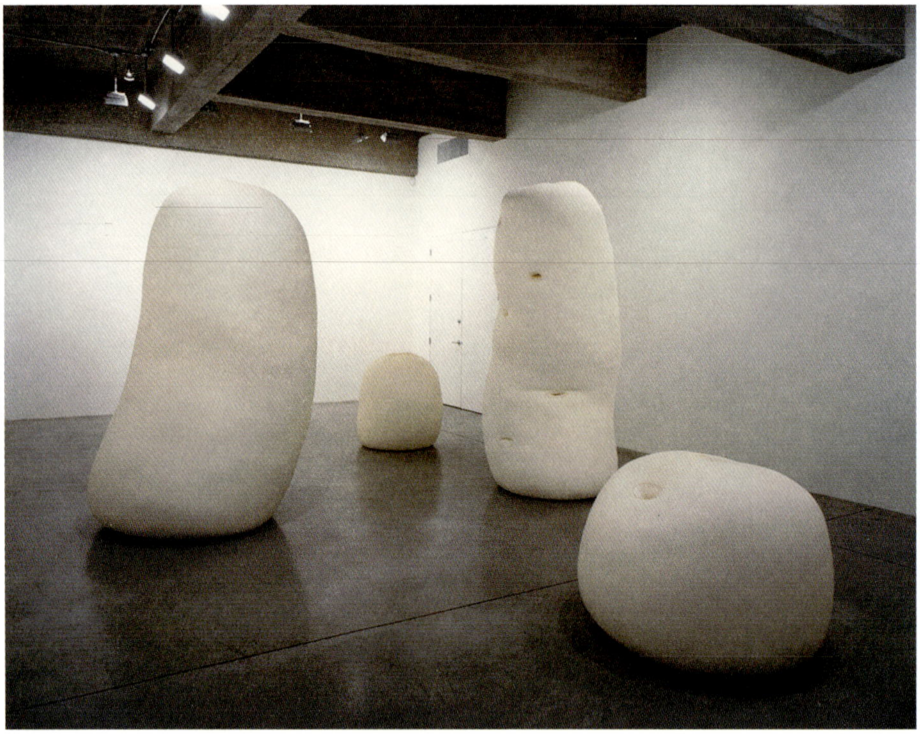

Ernesto Neto,
*The Ovaloids' Meeting,*
1998

ing the gestural works by "Action Painters" like Jackson Pollock. As well as being visually striking, the powders infuse the gallery with their potent scents, heightening the sensorial effect of the work.

While utilizing the same materials and similar forms as in *Piff, Paff, Puff*, much of Neto's recent work physically involves the viewer to a greater extent. *The Ovaloids Meeting* (1998) consists of several oval-shaped sculptures of white Lycra, approximately the average height of a person, which sit directly on the floor. Some of the *Ovaloids* have orifices that visitors can slip their hands and arms into, where they will feel the soft, tiny Styrofoam pellets that fill the sculptures. The *Ovaloids'* human scale and Neto's invitation to hug and investigate them anthropomorphize the sculptures, giving each one a distinct personality or character. The *Ovaloids* reflect the impact of fellow Brazilian artist Lygia Clark on Neto's work. Clark's influential work from the 1960s onward created the precedent for artwork that allows for active participation and has the potential for tangible, therapeutic effects. Through her relational objects—wearable masks, gloves, and body suits that people can pick up, put on, and play with—Clark aimed to make art that is simultaneously pleasurable and transformative. Neto similarly encourages a physical, as well as intellectual, interaction between the "viewer" and his sculptures.

Neto has also made a series of environments that people can walk into and be surrounded by—extending his interest in tactility and viewer interaction to a total body experience. Neto's *Nave Óvulo* (1998) is a cube of Lycra, suspended and stretched from its corners, with an opening at one end where visitors can climb into the piece. *Globiobabel Nudelione Landmoonaia* (2000) includes a forest of long, columnar pieces of fabric connecting the ceiling and the floor, interrupted by a massive Lycra pillow stuffed with Styrofoam pellets that viewers can sink into. Both sculptures conceive of the inner body on a macroscopic scale, allowing visitors to navigate through translucent, skinlike fabric and corporeal spaces reminiscent of bodily organs. These environments also play with the meaning of the word *nave*. In Portuguese, it can be translated as vessel; Neto's sculptures transport visitors, in both body and mind, to a cosmic, otherworldly landscape. In English, *nave* refers to the large open expanse of a cathedral's interior, often-quiet, awe-inspiring spaces. Neto's sculptures have a secular spirituality; much like churches, they are serene places that invite reflection and contemplation. In each of his environments and sculptures, Neto elegantly combines simple materials and sensual shapes to provide viewers with a playful, engaging, and stimulating experience.

EM

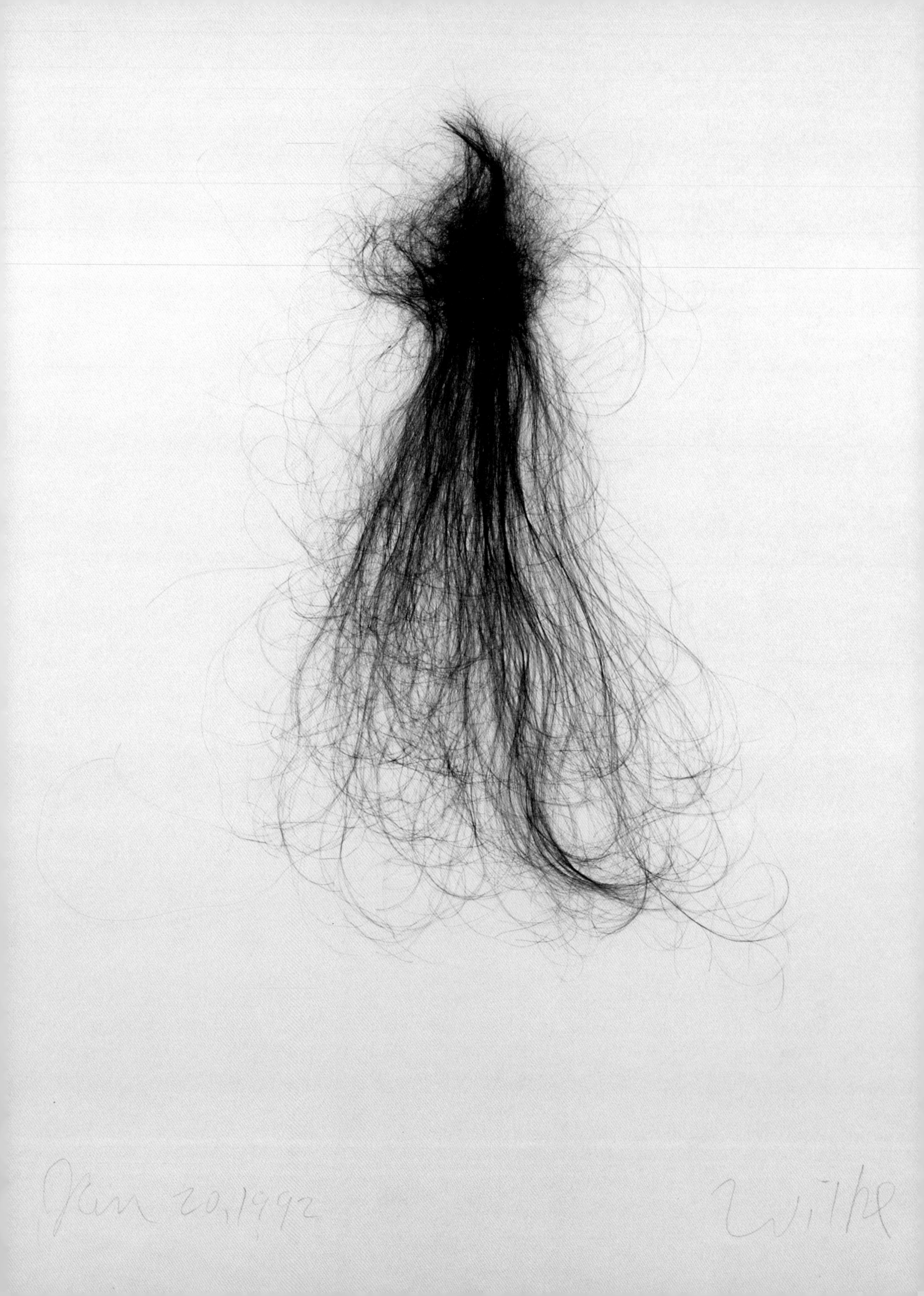
Jan 20, 1992

## HANNAH WILKE

Born in New York City, 1940. Died in Houston, Texas, 1993.

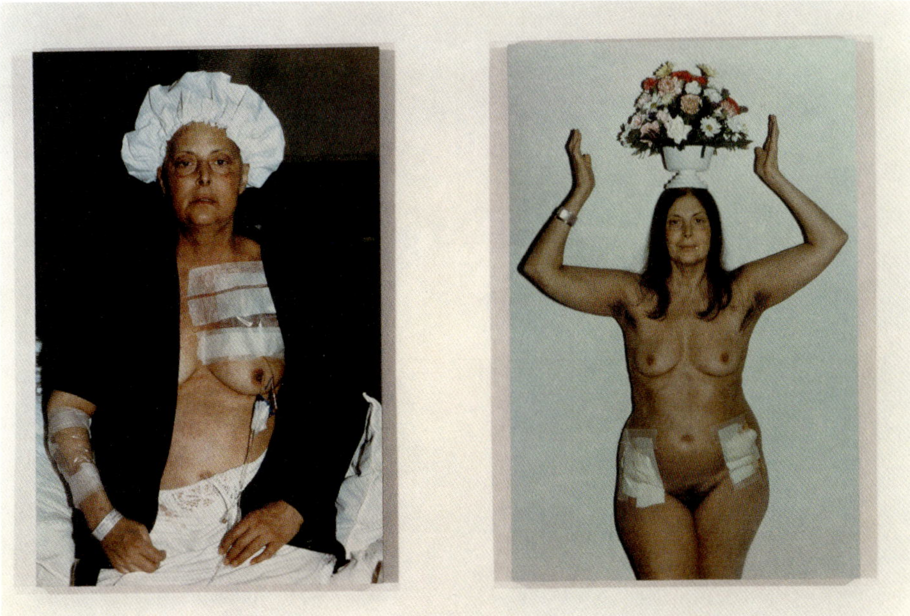

Hannah Wilke,
*June 15, 1992/*
*January 30, 1992:*
*#1 from INTRA-VENUS,*
1992-1993

Hannah Wilke's photographic diptych *So Help Me Hannah Series: Portrait of the Artist with Her Mother, Selma Butter* (1978-81) pictures Wilke photographed from above, bare-breasted and covered in tiny charms and miniature guns. Her face is made up dramatically—blue-green eye shadow, red cheeks and lips. She stares directly and defiantly at the camera. The right side of the work shows Wilke's mother, Selma, also nude from the waist up, revealing her scars from a mastectomy. The expression on her face is ambiguous, as she averts her eyes and face from the camera.

The work presents a stark comparison of daughter and mother, youth and age, health and illness, unabashed and wary nudity. For the four years before Selma's death in 1982, Wilke documented her mother's struggle with cancer. Wilke stated: "I took thousands of photographs of her ... hoping the images of her would keep her alive. ... The images I made of myself and my mother kept me alive."[1] The photograph can be seen as representative of both Wilke's early career—her provocative exploration of the depiction of the female body—and sadly, as a foreshadowing of the last series she would make, *Intra-Venus*, which records her battle with lymphoma. What links these two "bookends" of Wilke's career is what remained the same throughout all of her work—Wilke's use of her body as a way to challenge notions about art, femininity, the body, feminism, and politics.

Hannah Wilke,
*Brushstrokes:*
*January 20, 1992,*
1992

Wilke began using her nude body as the primary imagery of her performances and photography in 1970, after her mother's mastectomy. However, the female

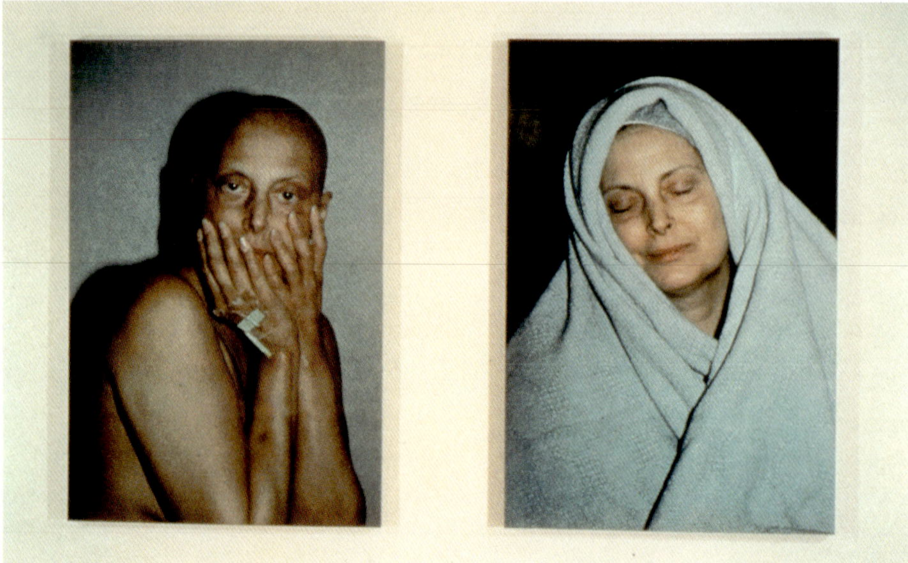

Hannah Wilke, *July 26, 1992/ February 19, 1992: #4 from INTRA-VENUS,* 1992-93

form was always essential to her work; Wilke's terra-cotta sculptures from the early 1960s, her "one-fold gestural objects," resemble abstracted vaginal forms. She continued using this shape throughout her career, as seen in *S.O.S—Starification Object Series* (1974), a group of photographs in which Wilke appears topless, striking different poses, many calling to mind the type of seductive looks that might be found in a fashion magazine. In each image, tiny pieces of folded chewing gum cover her body, the shape recalling a vulvar or scarlike form.

As with all of Wilke's work, *S.O.S.—Starification Object Series* is overtly feminist. Through her poses, she enacts the objectification and sexualization of women's bodies in both art and society. Women's bodies have often been the object of the male "gaze," especially the male artist's gaze, and yet women artists in the 1970s had only recently begun to use their own bodies as subject matter. The bubble gum sculptures act as tiny scars or wounds; Wilke once stated: "I chose gum because it's the perfect metaphor for the American woman—chew her up, get what you want out of her, throw her out and pop in a new piece."[2] While Wilke *objects* to the heritage of woman-as-(disposable) object, she also celebrates and flaunts her body, which, in many ways, fits a societal ideal. Because of this, critics have sometimes read Wilke's work as antithetical to feminist concerns, charging that it simply reenacts and reinforces the images of and notions about women that feminists have tried to reverse.

In 1987, Wilke was diagnosed with lymphoma. Until her death in 1993, she documented her struggle with the disease in a final series, *Intra-Venus. Intra-Venus*, which consists of large-scale color photographs, watercolor self-portraits, and sculptural objects made from Wilke's hair, is described by art historian Amelia Jones as "Wilke's brilliant riposte to those who condemned her work as narcissistic and Wilke herself as exploiting her own beauty."[3] In the diptych *June 15, 1992/January 30, 1992: #1 from INTRA-VENUS* Wilke is still posing nude for the camera, even though her once-thin, youthful body is bloated and ravaged from cancer treatments and medicines. In the left hand photograph she sits wearing a white shower cap, staring blankly at the viewer; one of her breasts is exposed through her hospital gown revealing a jumble of medical tape and intravenous needles. In the right photograph, Wilke comically poses with a vase of flowers on her head, holding her hands up as if she is a fertility goddess. Her hips are covered with gauze and tape, the reminders of a recent surgery.

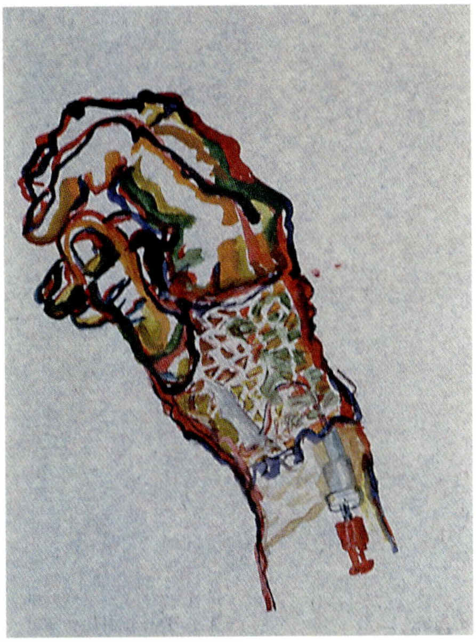

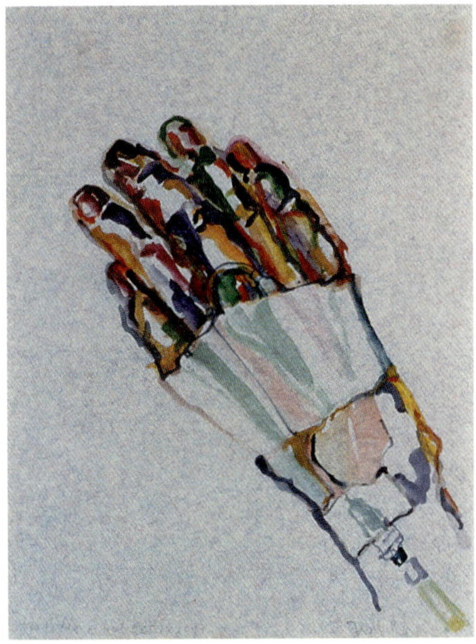

*left:*
Hannah Wilke,
*October 20, 1991: Hand #7 from INTRA-VENUS,*
1991

*right:*
Hannah Wilke,
*October 17, 1991: Hand #6 from INTRA-VENUS,*
1991

The photographs reflect the double meaning of the series' title. Wilke exposes her body as a passive object of both invasive medical procedures and the unrelenting course of the cancer. At the same time, in *Intra-Venus* Wilke continues to view her body as a viable site for an investigation of female representation and sexuality. While Hannah Wilke's physical appearance changed radically over her career, what stayed consistent was her unwavering gaze at all aspects of her self, life, and death and a belief in the power of her work to heal and transform.

EM

1 Joanna Frueh, "Hannah Wilke," *Hannah Wilke: A Retrospective* (Columbia, MO: University of Missouri Press, 1989), p. 150.
2 Avis Berman, "A Decade of Progress, but Could a Female Chardin Make a Living?" in *Art News*, no. 79 (October 1980), p. 77.
3 Amelia Jones, "Intra-Venus and Hannah Wilke's Feminist Narcissism," *Intra-Venus* (New York: Ronald Feldman Fine Arts, 1995), p. 9.

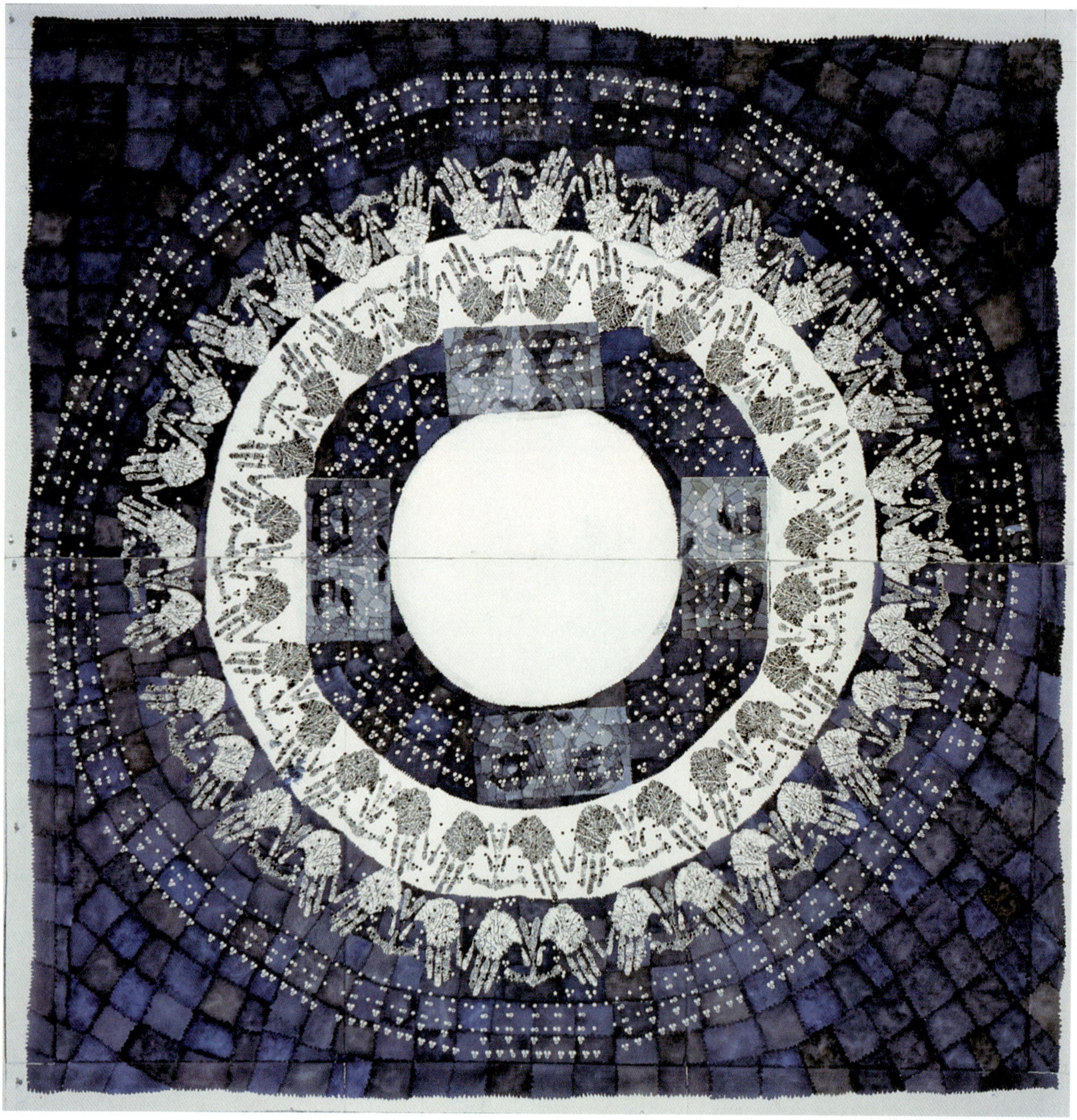

## RICHARD YARDE

Born in Boston, Massachusetts, 1939. Lives in Northampton, Massachusetts.

Richard Yarde's watercolors are grand in both size and conception. From the late 1960s through the 1980s, Yarde painted representational works based on his family history and youth in Boston, as well as on African American history and culture. His paintings depict some of his heroes: famous politicians, singers, and entertainers like Malcolm X, Marcus Garvey, Josephine Baker, and boxer Jack Johnson. In 1982, he made *Savoy,* a sculptural installation recreating the famous Savoy Ballroom of Harlem, a dancehall that flourished from 1926 until 1956. Inspired primarily by black and white photographs of the club, Yarde's *Savoy* brings the dancers, musicians, and décor of the ballroom to life in vibrant colors and pattern. For these early paintings of the people and places that shaped his identity, Yarde drew his imagery from a fusion of photographs, experience, popular culture, and his personal, as well as cultural, memory.

In 1991, Yarde suffered from kidney failure, an illness brought on by years of taking high blood pressure medication, and one that nearly killed him. The experience radically impaired his speech and mobility; a series of mini-strokes left him without feeling in his hands, a loss particularly devastating for an artist. After a year of rehabilitation, Yarde regained enough ability to return to his studio, where his work took on a dramatic new appearance, reflecting the transformative nature of the disease on his life. Moving away from representational images of historical figures or cultural history, Yarde's work over the past ten years has become an abstract, mystical expression of his dreams and experiences with both illness and healing.

*Mojo Hand* (1995-1996) marks Yarde's transition toward a new artistic sensibility and presents the imagery and motifs that have appeared in his work since: dot patterns, X-rays, disembodied hands and heads. Yarde combines these new elements with those that have been consistent throughout his oeuvre—a gridlike background of irregularly shaped squares of color and a prominent use of the color indigo. An X-ray of a pregnant woman, surrounded by handprints, dominates the center of *Mojo Hand.* To the left of the X-ray, Yarde painted a double helix of DNA— the blueprint for human life. To the right, there is a series of dots—the 23rd Psalm ("The Lord is my Shepard; I shall not want...") written in Braille; the prayer was Yarde's mantra as he struggled to regain his health. The painting, particularly Yarde's use of his handprint, refers to the many modes of healing that Yarde turned to as he waited for a kidney transplant (which he received in 2000). In addition to traditional medical treatment, Yarde looked to alternative medicines, particularly those that use touch as an essential element, such as massage and chiropractic work. Furthermore, in many cultures and religions—from African American hoodoo to Catholicism—hands, both literally and

*left page:*
Richard Yarde,
*Pulse,*
2000–2001

iconographically, are protective and healing devices. Ultimately, *Mojo Hand* embodies the self-healing in Yarde's return to the studio and the therapeutic nature of making something with one's hands.

*Pulse* (2000-2001), one in a recent series of paintings with the circle as the common motif, also features Yarde's handprints and a dot pattern; both form concentric rings around a central, white circle, which for Yarde represents a divination tray. Divination trays are ritual objects used traditionally in many African cultures for foretelling the future, giving meaning to an event, or aiding in decision making. It is the space where the human and spirit worlds unite and communicate. In *Pulse*, the "divination tray" is bordered by four self-portraits of Yarde's eyes and nose, mimicking the customary decoration of many divination trays, which depict gods along their edge. Unlike *Mojo Hand, Pulse*'s dot patterns are scientific rather than spiritual. They are based on a coding of neutrons and protons colliding to produce helium in the sun. For Yarde, the pattern represents an "energy shift," perhaps symbolizing his own energy shift after surviving kidney failure and a transplant. Both *Pulse* and *Mojo Hand* display the dynamic interaction of the multiple forces that have informed Yarde's recent work: faith and medicine; spirituality and science; religion and ritual; modernity and tradition. While rooted in personal experience, Yarde's paintings are universal explorations of the complex nature of illness and healing.

EM

## COPYRIGHT AND PHOTO CREDITS

**Pulse: Art, Healing, and Transformation** is made possible by an Emily Hall Tremaine Exhibition Award. Major funding has also been provided by The Andy Warhol Foundation for the Visual Arts. The exhibition is sponsored by Harvard Pilgrim Health Care Foundation. Additional support has been provided by the Boston Office of Cultural Affairs/Boston Cultural Agenda Fund and the Goethe Institut Boston.

Harvard Pilgrim Health Care Foundation

MAYOR THOMAS M. MENINO
WWW.CITYOFBOSTON.GOV/ARTS
BOSTON NOW

**First Edition published 2003 by ICA and Steidl Publishers**

Editor: Jessica Morgan

Curatorial Assistant: Emily Moore

Copy editor: Matthew Abbate

Translations: Arthur Goldhammer

Catalogue for an exhibition held at the Institute of Contemporary Art, Boston
May 14–August 31, 2003


Thierry Davila's essays were first published in *L'Art Médicine*,
Réunion des Musées Nationaux, 1999 in French
Design: Steidl Design / Claas Möller

Printing and scans by Steidl
Düstere Strasse 4
D-37073 Göttingen
Phone: ++49 551 496060
Fax: ++49 551 4960649

Distributed by D.A.P., Distributed Art Publishers, Inc.
155 Avenue of the Americas
Second Floor
New York, NY 10013-1507, USA
Phone: 212 627 1999
Fax: 212 627 9484

ISBN 0-910663-64-5
ISBN 3-88243-922-X (Steidl)